America's Founding Fathers and the Bible

A Select Study of America's Christian Origin

Stephen A. Flick, Ph.D.

WESTBOW
P R E S S®
A DIVISION OF THOMAS NELSON
& ZONDERVAN

WestBow Press books may be ordered through booksellers or by contacting:

WestBow Press
A Division of Thomas Nelson & Zondervan
1663 Liberty Drive
Bloomington, IN 47403
www.westbowpress.com
1 (866) 928-1240

ISBN: 978-1-5127-6112-2 (sc)
ISBN: 978-1-5127-6113-9 (hc)
ISBN: 978-1-5127-6111-5 (e)

Library of Congress Control Number: 2016917592

Print information available on the last page.

WestBow Press rev. date: 1/3/2017

CONTENTS

Image Credits

Cover: George Washington, by Gilbert Stuart - Metropolitan Museum of Art, Public Domain

King James I, by Daniel Mytens, Wikimedia Commons, Public domain

Maximilien de Robespierre, by Unknown (French school), Wikimedia Commons, Public Domain

David Josiah Brewer, Author Unknown, Wikimedia Commons, Public Domain

John Hancock, by John Singleton Copley, Wikimedia Commons, Public Domain

Henry Laurens, by Lemuel Francis Abbott, Wikipedia, Public Domain

Woodrow Wilson, by Frank Graham Cootes, Wikimedia Commons, Public Domain

Early Printing Press, by Daniel Chodowiecki, Wikimedia Commons, Public Domain

Dr. Patrick Allison Church, (Boulden, James E. P. The Presbyterians of Baltimore; Their Churches and Historic Grave-Yards. Baltimore: W. J. Boyle & son, 1875).

First Prayer in Congress, by T.H. Matheson, Wikimedia Commons, Public Domain

John Jay, by Gilbert Stuart - The National Gallery of Art, Public Domain

Death of George Washington, in *Life of George Washington: The Christian*, lithograph by Claude Regnier, after Junius Brutus Stearns,1853; Library of Congress Prints and Photographs Division

Portrait of Franklin, by Joseph Siffred Duplessis, Wikimedia Commons, Public Domain

Benjamin Franklin (center) at work on a printing press. Reproduction of a Charles Mills painting by the Detroit Publishing Company, Wikimedia Commons, Public Domain

Declaration of Independence [Committee of Five], John Trumbull, Wikimedia Commons, Public Domain

Thomas Paine, by Matthew Pratt, Wikimedia Commons, Public Domain

Benjamin Rush, by Charles Willson Peale, Wikimedia Commons, Public Domain

John Knox Witherspoon, artist unknown, Wikimedia Commons, Public Domain

Signing of Declaration of Independence, by Armand-Dumaresq, Wikimedia Commons, Public Domain

John Wesley, by Frank O. Salisbury, Wikimedia Commons, Public Domain

Bishop Asbury, engraving, Public Domain

Voltaire (Francois-Marie Arouet), by Maurice Quentin de La Tour, Wikimedia Commons, Public Domain

John Adams, by Asher B. Durand, Wikimedia Commons, Public Domain

Timothy Dwight, by John Trumbull, Wikimedia Commons, Public Domain

Jacob Duche, unknown artist, Wikimedia Commons, Public Domain

Eleazar Lord, from *Between the Ocean and the Lakes: The Story of Erie*, by Edward Harold Mott, Wikimedia Commons, Public Domain

John Pollock, by John F. Francis, John Rudy Photography and Pennsylvania Capitol Preservation Committee

Elias Boudinot IV, by Charles Willson Peale, Wikimedia Commons, Public Domain

Federal Hall and Trinity Church 1789, Wikimedia Commons, Public Domain

William Jay, artist unknown, Wikimedia Commons, Public Domain

Robert Charles Winthrop, by Daniel Huntington, Collection of the U.S. House of Representatives, Public Domain

Daniel Webster, by N. Currier, Wikimedia Commons, Public Domain

INTRODUCTION

The United States of America arose out of its fledgling origin of thirteen English colonies scattered along the Atlantic seaboard. Although the term "Virginia" is most commonly associated with the state that bears this name, originally this term applied to an area along the Atlantic seaboard that covered an area roughly extending from the current southern border of Canada through South Carolina—an area much larger than the state of Virginia itself.

From the middle of the twentieth century, Americans have been told that their nation arose out of the barrenness of secularism. However, nothing could be further from the truth. In fact, those making such claims—including many in American academia, jurisprudence, and other disciplines—by default admit their ignorance of the facts when they seek to advance their secular propaganda.

On April 10, 1606, the Virginia Company was chartered by England's King James I for the purpose of establishing English settlements along the eastern coast of North America. Contrary to secularists' claims that the primary motive of colonialization of these territories was commercial, King James made it clear that the primary interest behind this endeavor was the advancement of the Gospel. In

King James I

the "First Virginia Charter," King James' Christian motivation behind granting permission to settle in the New World occupied a place of prominence:

> We, greatly commending, and graciously accepting of, their Desires for the Furtherance of so noble a Work, which may, by the Providence of Almighty God, hereafter tend to the Glory of his Divine Majesty, in propagating of Christian Religion to such People, as yet live in Darkness and miserable Ignorance of the true Knowledge and Worship of God, and may in time bring the Infidels and Savages, living in those parts, to human Civility, and to a settled and quiet Government: DO, by these our Letters Patents, graciously accept of, and agree to, their humble and well-intended Desires.[1]

Not only did the First Virginia Charter contain the Christian motivation behind the English settlements in the New World, but all of the charters and constitutions of the Thirteen Colonies that emerged confessed allegiance to and dependence upon biblical Christianity for their principles and practices of government. Secularists and their fellow irreligionists can find no historical basis to advocate the notion that the foundation of American government during the colonial era, or later under the Constitution, was founded upon godless principles.[2] Rather, both private and public writings overwhelmingly demonstrate that America's Founding Fathers intended and did establish American government upon biblical principles and practices.

---

[1] "The First Virginia Constitution," *Declaration of Independence* (http://www.ushistory.org/declaration/related/vaconst.htm, July 7, 2015).

[2] For a good documentary presentation on the Christian origin of colonial America's Christian origin, please see, William J. Federer, *The Original 13: A Documentary History of Religion in America's First Thirteen States* (St. Louis, MO: Amerisearch, Inc., 2007), 12:407.

The secular mantra, "Religion and government never mix," is misinformed. To be more precise, the position of "Wrong religion and irreligion never mix," is historically accurate. While the irreligious and secular seek to point to dark periods of Christian history for justification of their argument against Christian influence in government, their position is an appeal to error. Just because a medical doctor

Maximilien de Robespierre

abuses the correct practice of medicine is no justification for rejecting the use of correct medical principles. Just as there may be degrees of deviation from the correct observance of every practice, so there are deviations from true religion. The first significant secular state was the result of the French Revolution. The horrific blood-letting of this godless secular state was widely rehearsed throughout America at the time it occurred, but in recent decades the irreligious intellectual descendants of Robespierre and other leaders of the French Revolution refuse to discuss these facts. And, the social instability that the French Revolution caused the nation of France has been remarkable, resulting in nearly a dozen and a half constitutions and governments since that time. Compare this to the fact that America has had only one Constitution during the same period of time!

Above all nations throughout world history, America has most closely reflected the teachings of Christianity to national life, and the reason is the place that the Bible was accorded at its inception. A careful study of American history from Jamestown and Plymouth throughout the Revolutionary War and Constitutional eras will disclose a wealth of proofs that America was founded as a Christian nation, upon the principles of the Bible. While the faithful historian is capable of producing a stream of evidence in support of this truth from the era of the earliest English settlements to demonstrate the critical role the Bible was accorded in the birth and development of America, skeptics could yet respond, "We do not live under the forms of government created by the Pilgrims and Puritans; we live under the government of the United States Constitution, and for this reason, a discussion of the English settlement of America has little or no relevance to a contemporary understanding of American government. After all, the Constitution was written more than a century and a half after the Pilgrims and Puritans landed in the New World."

Given the fact that American government prior to the Constitution was very different than that which emerged following its ratification, this work will not preoccupy itself with the earliest influences of Christianity upon American government. While volumes of evidence may be produced to demonstrate the guiding influence that Christianity and the Bible exercised upon America's government from the earliest eras of English settlement, this work will confine itself to the era of the American Revolution and following. This brief work is not intended to be exhaustive, but rather descriptive of the influence which Christianity exercised upon the formation of America as an independent nation. It is the author's intent to sufficiently expose the historical facts concerning the use of the Bible by the Founding Fathers to deny the irreligious their boast that, "America was established as a secular nation." While mountains of evidence refute this argument of secularists, the place the Bible occupied in the thought and practice of the Founding Fathers during the American Revolution and Constitutional era is sufficient to refute such uninformed professions.

THE CONTINENTAL CONGRESS AND THE BIBLE

B ecause of the limited scope of this work, opportunity does not allow an extended discussion of many significant subjects that—when coupled with more detailed information—must necessarily produce tomes of writings defending the Christian origin of America. This fact is supported by the finding of the United States Supreme Court at the end of the nineteenth century. After presenting more than eighty pieces of evidence of America's Christian origin, Supreme Court Justice, David Brewer—writing the majority decision for a unanimous court—arrived at this same conclusion in 1892: ". . . many other matters which might be noticed, add a volume of unofficial declarations to the mass of organic utterances that this is a Christian nation."[3] In his classic work, *The Christian Life and Character of the Civil Institutions of the United States,*[4] Benjamin F. Morris discusses the numerous rulings and studies of the Supreme Court, Congress,

David Josiah Brewer

---

[3] The United States Supreme Court Vs. Holy Trinity Church v. U.S. 143 U.S. 457, 12 S.Ct. 511, 36 L.Ed. 226 Feb. 29, 1892 (http://supreme.justia.com/us/143/457/case.html, November 21, 2011).

[4] For a very good survey of this, please see Benjamin Morris, *Christian Life and Character of the Civil Institutions of the United States, Developed in the Official*

and other governmental agencies that clearly recount these institutions' conclusion that America "is a Christian nation." For the sake of brevity, the discussion of this section will limit itself to several proofs of the Christian convictions of America's Founding Fathers as primarily expressed in the decisions of the Continental Congress, or those years immediately prior to America winning her independence. From this era, we will further limit ourselves to two subjects—fasting and thanksgiving days and the Continental Congress' regard for the Bible.

Fasting and Thanksgiving Days Proclaimed

One of the many proofs of America's Christian origin is the Christian worship that its government has encouraged. One of the forms of worship encouraged by America's state and national governments has been "fasting and thanksgiving days." While it is true that the Pilgrims were the first to formally call for a time of thanksgiving to God for his bountiful provision in the harvest of 1621, it became a custom in the governments of the individual thirteen English American colonies to call for days of "fasting" as well as days of "thanksgiving." The first fast day was observed in Plymouth Colony in 1636 with other Puritan colonies soon following this example. During the American Revolution, other colonies also proclaimed fast days.

In addition to colonial use of fast days, the Continental Congress (1774-1789) also made use of both fast and thanksgiving proclamations. The Continental Congress acted similarly to the federal government under the United States Constitution (beginning in 1789). Just as the individual colonies had proclaimed days of fasting and thanksgiving, so the Continental Congress assumed the practice of proclaiming similar

---

and Historical Annals of the Republic (Philadelphia: George W. Childs, 1864), 306-332.

For a reprint of this class work, please see Benjamin F. Morris, *The Christian Life and Character of the Civil Institutions of the United States.* 2nd (Powder Springs GA: American Vision, 2007) 367-404.

days. Speaking of "fast and thanksgiving days," one historian noted the significance of such proclamations:

> This national custom has a Divine origin and sanction, and was designed, and is eminently adapted, to give religious culture to the national heart and conscience and to exert a beneficent influence on the civil and religious interests of a people.[5]

Far from being secularists, deists, atheists, agnostics or any other form of irreligion, the leaders of the Continental Congress were deeply committed Christians. In the following pages, examples of fast day and thanksgiving day proclamations by Congress are provided to enable the reader to appreciate the extent to which America's Founding Fathers sought to engraft some of the principles of the Bible into national practice. For the sake of clarity, readers are advised that these extended quotes are taken from the minutes or *Journals of the Continental Congress, 1774-1789.*

Beginning of Fast Days Under Continental Congress

On June 12, 1775, the Continental Congress issued one of its first fast day proclamations when John Hancock of Massachusetts was president of Congress.[6] Hancock, one of the wealthiest Americans of his day, was the son and grandson of

John Hancock

---

[5] Morris, *Civil Institutions of the United States*, 525.

[6] John Hancock was the longest serving president of the Continental Congress, serving on two occasions, from May 24, 1775 to October 29, 1777 and from November 23, 1785 to June 5, 1786—a total of 1085 days. "President of the Continental Congress," *Wikipedia* (https://en.wikipedia.org/wiki/President_of_the_Continental_Congress, November 18, 2015).

Christian ministers and was personally a deeply committed Christian. Under the above date, the *Journals of Congress* records the following fast day resolution:

> The committee, appointed for preparing a resolve for a fast, brought in a report, which, being read, was agreed to as follows:
>
> As the great Governor of the World, by his supreme and universal Providence, not only conducts the course of nature with unerring wisdom and rectitude, but frequently influences the minds of men to serve the wise and gracious purposes of his providential government; and it being, at all times, our indispensable duty devoutly to acknowledge his superintending providence, especially in times of impending danger and public calamity, to reverence and adore his immutable justice as well as to implore his merciful interposition for our deliverance:
>
> This Congress, therefore, considering the present critical, alarming and calamitous state of these colonies, do earnestly recommend that Thursday, the 20th day of July next, be observed, by the inhabitants of all the English colonies on this continent, as a day of public humiliation, fasting and prayer; that we may, with united hearts and voices, unfeignedly confess and deplore our many sins; and offer up our joint supplications to the all-wise, omnipotent, and merciful Disposer of all events; humbly beseeching him to forgive our iniquities, to remove our present calamities, to avert those desolating judgments, with which we are threatened, and to bless our rightful sovereign, King George the third, and [to] inspire him with wisdom to discern and pursue the true interest

of all his subjects, that a speedy end may be put to the civil discord between Great Britain and the American colonies, without farther effusion of blood: And that the British nation may be influenced to regard the things that belong to her peace, before they are hid from her eyes: That these colonies may be ever under the care and protection of a kind Providence, and be prospered in all their interests; That the divine blessing may descend and rest upon all our civil rulers, and upon the representatives of the people, in their several assemblies and conventions, that they may be directed to wise and effectual measures for preserving the union, and securing the just rights and privileges of the colonies; That virtue and true religion may revive and flourish throughout our land; And that all America may soon behold a gracious interposition of Heaven, for the redress of her many grievances, the restoration of her invaded rights, a reconciliation with the parent state, on terms constitutional and honorable to both; And that her civil and religious privileges may be secured to the latest posterity.

And it is recommended to Christians, of all denominations, to assemble for public worship, and to abstain from servile labor and recreations on said day.

Ordered, That a copy of the above be signed by the president and attested by the Secy [Secretary] and published in the newspapers, and in hand bills.[7]

It may be noted from the quote above that the general terms used at this point in American history to refer to God and his activity in the world—such as "the great Governor of the World, by his supreme and

---

[7] Orthography updated in quote. *Journals of the Continental Congress, 1774-1789*, ed. Worthington C. Ford, et al (Washington, D.C.: 1904), 2:87-88.

universal Providence"—were used to refer to the Christian God of the Bible, as clearly indicated by the literary context of this proclamation— the proclamation being "recommended to Christians, of all denominations." The argument used by secularists to suggest that such general references to God reflected the influence of deism is ill-informed and indifferent to literary and historical facts. Because eleven of the thirteen colonies had instituted state controlled churches, the earliest beginnings of America's federal government—as seen here in the Continental Congress—used general terms acceptable to all Christians when referring to God to avoid needless controversy. With this fact well established from the *Journals of the Continental Congress*, the notion that the United States Constitution was a "godless" document is historically uninformed.[8] In an effort to maintain unity to receive sufficient votes to ratify the Constitution among the states following the Revolution, religious matters and the terms used to discuss them were left to the individual states—something to which the Supreme Court has been indifferent since the 1940s.

Beginning of Thanksgiving Days Under Continental Congress

In addition to calling the American Colonies to the Christian practice of fasting, the Continental Congress observed yet another Christian discipline—formal religious expressions of thanksgiving. Though thanksgiving proclamations had

Henry Laurens

---

[8] In 1996, two Cornell University professors, Isaac Kramnick and R. Laurence Moore, argued that the framers of the United States Constitution "created an utterly secular state." Obviously Kramnick and Moore were ignorant to the roots of the federalism found in the Continental Congress—the consequence of failing to do their historical homework! See Isaac Kramnick and R. Laurence Moore, *The Godless Constitution: The Case against Religious Correctness*, 1st ed. (New York: Norton, 1996).

been initiated by the individual colonies, they were accorded collective or "federal" practice during the Continental Congress, which was America's first attempt at a unified form of government. One of the first thanksgiving proclamations was issued by Congress on Saturday, November 1, 1777, under the leadership of the newly elected President, Henry Laurens of South Carolina. The clear biblical influence upon the recommendation presented to Congress is evident in the minutes of Congress:

> The committee appointed to prepare a recommendation to these states, to set apart a day of thanksgiving, brought in a report; which was agreed to as follows:

> Forasmuch as it is the indispensable duty of all men to adore the superintending providence of Almighty God; to acknowledge with gratitude their obligation to him for benefits received, and to implore such farther blessings as they stand in need of; and it having pleased him in his abundant mercy not only to continue to us the innumerable bounties of his common providence, but also to smile upon us in the prosecution of a just and necessary war, for the defense and establishment of our unalienable rights and liberties; particularly in that he hath been pleased in so great a measure to prosper the means used for the support of our troops and to crown our arms with most signal success: It is therefore recommended to the legislative or executive powers of these United States, to set apart Thursday, the eighteenth day of December next, for solemn thanksgiving and praise; that with one heart and one voice the good people may express the grateful feelings of their hearts, and consecrate themselves to the service of their divine benefactor; and that together with their sincere acknowledgments and offerings, they may join the

penitent confession of their manifold sins, whereby they had forfeited every favor, and their humble and earnest supplication that it may please God, through the merits of Jesus Christ, mercifully to forgive and blot them out of remembrance; that it may please him graciously to afford his blessing on the governments of these states respectively, and prosper the public council of the whole; to inspire our commanders both by land and sea, and all under them, with that wisdom and fortitude which may render them fit instruments, under the providence of Almighty God, to secure for these United States the greatest of all human blessings, independence and peace; that it may please him to prosper the trade and manufactures of the people and the labor of the husbandman, that our land may yet yield its increase; to take schools and seminaries of education, so necessary for cultivating the principles of true liberty, virtue and piety, under his nurturing hand, and to prosper the means of religion for the promotion and enlargement of that kingdom which consisteth "in righteousness, peace and joy in the Holy Ghost."[9]

Who can read such biblically and theologically ladened records and seriously deny the Christian influence the Founding Fathers sought to exert upon America. Yet since the middle of the twentieth century, judges, educators, the media, and many other persons and groups have done just that!

Fast and thanksgiving day proclamations of the Continental Congress were distributed to the individual states with the request "that servile labor, and such recreation as, though at other times innocent, may be unbecoming the purpose of this appointment, be omitted on so solemn

---

[9] Orthography updated in quote. *Journals of the Continental Congress,* 7:854-855.

an occasion."[10] The appeals of Congress concerning these days were recommendations "to Christians of all denominations,"[11] and to ensure that these proclamations would be widely observed, they were "published in the newspapers, and in hand bills."[12] These were not recommendations to other religions outside the Christian faith. When Congress used the term "religion", it was a reference to Christianity in general, without concern to a specific Christian denomination. It was the custom of Congress, when issuing proclamations for fast or thanksgiving days, to suspend business for the days they had appointed for special observance of fasting or thanksgiving. Even the American Continental Army observed the fast and thanksgiving proclamations of Congress. Unlike the secularism that has come to characterize a significant portion of America's contemporary military, "the army under Washington observed . . . [fast and thanksgiving days] with devout reverence."[13]

Proclamations concerning fast and thanksgiving days continued long after the establishment of America as an independent nation. Fast day proclamations and observances continued into the twentieth century when in 1918 Woodrow Wilson proclaimed a national fast day with the support of the Congress.[14] Thanksgiving days were employed long before the Continental Congress decided to make use of them, but once it did, it was not ashamed to justify their use from Scripture. Thanksgiving days were proclaimed by the Continental Congress in 1777, 1779, 1780, 1781, and 1782, to say

Woodrow Wilson

[10] *Journals of the Continental Congress,* 7:855.

[11] Orthography updated in quote. *Journals of the Continental Congress,* 2:87-88.

[12] *Journals of the Continental Congress,* 2:88.

[13] Morris, *Civil Institutions of the United States,* 527.

[14] M. Payne, "Fast Days," *Christianity in America.* eds. Daniel Reid, et al (Downers Grove, IL: InterVarsity Press, 1990).

nothing of their use by Presidents Washington, Adams, and beyond. But what does this brief study of fast days and thanksgiving days found in the *Journals of Congress* tell us concerning America's religious heritage? That question is aptly summarized in the following quote from historian, Benjamin F. Morris:

> These official state papers are rich in Christian doctrines, and confirm the great truth that the religion of the fathers of the Revolution and the founders of our civil Governments was the religion of the Bible. The proclamations issued by Congress make known the religious sentiments and feelings of the members of Congress, and constitute a rich part of the political Christian literature of the republic.[15]

Congress Advocates the Use of the Bible

Printers in the American Colonies were prohibited from printing any English Bibles by governmental decree. Only three British printing establishments were permitted to participate in this lucrative business—the University Presses of Oxford and Cambridge and one additional printer designated by the King. Controlling who printed the Bible helped to ensure the accuracy of the English

Early Printing

Bible and also provided a very profitable income for the three printing establishments. Though New England printers were permitted to print Bibles for certain Indians tribes and German Bibles, the printing of English Bibles was strictly forbidden.[16] As a result, when the American

---

[15] Morris, *Civil Institutions of the United States*, 527-528.

[16] *Unholy Hands on the Bible*. ed. Jay P. Green (Lafayette IN: Sovereign Grace Trust Fund, 1992), 432.

Revolution began, the supply of Bibles to America was cut-off, creating an enormous need for Scripture in the Thirteen United States.

In July 1777, the Continental Congress responded to a request placed before it by three clergymen, Francis Alison, John Ewing, and William Marshalle. Rev. Alison was a distinguished minister who assisted Benjamin Franklin with the development of the College of Philadelphia (today known as the University of Pennsylvania) and was instrumental in the formation of the University of Delaware. Rev. Ewing was the provost of the College of Philadelphia, and Rev. Marshalle was a minister in the Scots Presbyterian Church, part of the Presbytery of Pennsylvania. The three ministers asked Congress to undertake the printing of an inexpensive form of the Bible that would meet the ever-growing need for Scripture. Their letter to the Continental Congress clearly outlined their request:

> To the honorable Continental Congress of the United States of North America now sitting in Philadelphia.
>
> Honored Gentlemen,
>
> We the ministers of the Gospel of Christ in the City of Philadelphia, whose names are under written, taking it into our serious consideration that in our present circumstances, books in general, and in particular, the Holy Scriptures contained in the Old and New Testaments are growing so scarce and dear, that we greatly fear that unless timely care be used to prevent it, we shall not have Bibles for our schools and families, and for the public worship of God in our churches.
>
> We therefore think it our duty to our country and to the churches of Christ to lay this danger before this honorable house, humbly requesting that under your care, and by your encouragement, a copy of the

Holy Bible may be printed, so as to be sold nearly as cheap as the common Bibles, formerly imported from Britain and Ireland, were sold.

The number of purchasers is so great, that we doubt not but a large impression would soon be sold, but unless the sale of the whole edition belong to the printer, and he be bound under sufficient penalties, that no copy be sold by him, nor by any retailer under him, at a higher price than that allowed by this honorable house, we fear that the whole impression would soon be bought up, and sold again at an exorbitant price, which would frustrate your pious endeavors and fill the country with just complaints.

We are persuaded that your care and seasonable interposition will remove the anxious fears of many pious and well-disposed persons; would prevent the murmurs of the discontented; would save much money to the United States; would be the means of promoting Christian knowledge in our churches, and would transmit your names with additional honor to the latest posterity.

Our sincere prayers shall ever be for your welfare and prosperity, and we beg leave with the greatest respect to subscribe ourselves.

Honored Gentlemen,
Your most obedient humble servants,
Francis Alison
John Ewing
William Marshalle[17]

---

[17] The source from which this quote was derived was provided by Margaret T. Hills, former Secretary for Research of The American Bible Society. "The First

The primary request from the three clergymen was that "a copy of the holy Bible may be printed, so as to be sold nearly as cheap as the common Bibles, formerly imported from Britain and Ireland." This was the first request for a domestic printing of the English Bible in America. The Continental Congress made no appeal to "separation of church and state" as fraudulent interpreters

Dr. Patrick Allison's Church

of American history would now have the world believe. Rather, its Presbyterian chaplain, Rev. Dr. Patrick Allison (personal friend of George Washington),[18] brought the matter immediately to the attention of Congress for action.[19] So urgent was the matter that Congress took

---

American Bible," *Logos Resource Pages* (http://logosresourcepages.org/Versions/1st. htm, November 19, 2015).

[18] The Rev. Dr. Patrick Allison (1740 to August 21, 1802) was born in Franklin (or what was then known as Lancaster) County, Pennsylvania in 1740. He graduated from the College of Philadelphia (later the University of Pennsylvania) in 1760 and soon after was appointed Professor in the Academy of Newark, Delaware. In March 1763, he was licensed to preach by the Second Presbytery of Philadelphia in March 1763. In August of that same year, he was invited to minister at a newly formed congregation in Baltimore and was subsequently ordained as its pastor in 1765. After beginning the church in private homes clustered around the Inner Harbor, the congregation moved to a log church in 1763, then to a brick church in 1765, and subsequently to a spacious two-steeple church in 1790. Here he continued to minister for thirty-five years until his death on August 21, 1802. Dr. Allison was also the Chaplain to the Continental Congress and personal friend of George Washington. "Biographical Index of Ministers — A," *Presbyterian Heritage Center* (http://www.phcmontreat.org/bios/ Bios-A.htm, November 20, 2015); "Our History," *First & Franklin Presbyterian Church* (http://www.firstfranklin.org/index.php/about/history/, November 20, 2015).

[19] For Chaplain Allison's role in bringing it to the attention of Congress, see, Bill Federer, "Bible of the Revolution: Among Rarest of Books," *WND* (http://www.wnd.com/2015/07/bible-of-the-revolution-among-rarest-of-books/#jmyayl7hjpd2w5TU.99, November 19, 2015).

up the request from the three clergymen the same day[20]—Monday July 7, 1777—and appointed a committee of three members of the Continental Congress to look into the matter. The members of the committee appointed by the Continental Congress were Daniel Roberdeau, John Adams, and Jonathan Bayard Smith.[21]

From all indication, the three-member committee of Congress began its work immediately. They composed a list of issues to be addressed to see if it was feasible to print Bibles in America. Once this list of issues was composed, they sent their points of enquiry to printers in the Philadelphia area, including Henry Miller, Robert Aitken, Thomas Bradford, John Dunlap, and William Sellers.[22] The specific questions they wished to have answered by the printers were,

1. How many thousand pounds of types would be sufficient to set, or compose a whole Bible of the common sort; and what they would cost?
2. In how long time such a Bible could be set & printed?
3. What it could be sold for, as well bound, as our common Bibles?
4. Whether paper fit for the purpose, & a sufficient quantity of it could be had in this country, so as to carry on the work with expedition?
5. How long the types when set would continue good, and fit for this purpose of casting off a new edition from time to time?
6. What would be expected from the Congress to carry on this work, that it might be well done & sold nearly as cheap as common school Bible?

---

[20] *Letters of Delegates to Congress, 1774-1789*, ed. Paul H. Smith, et al. (Washington, D.C.: Library of Congress, 1976), 7:311.

[21] *Journals of the Continental Congress*, 8:536

[22] *Letters of Delegates to Congress*, 7:311.

An answer to these queries is requested against Friday at 6 o clock in the afternoon-to be given to the Committee of the Congress at the state house in this city. [23]

More than two months after accepting their assignment, the three-member Bible committee, on September 11, 1777, submitted their recommendations to Congress based upon the information they had received from the printers of Philadelphia. Because of the expense and various considerations involved in printing a Bible in America, it was recommended that Congress purchase Bibles through foreign sources wherever they could be found—rather than attempting to print them at that time. In the *Journals of Congress*, we read their report:

First Prayer in Congress

The committee appointed to consider the memorial [or request] of the Rev. Dr. Allison and others [the three Philadelphia clergymen originally submitting the request], report, "That they have conferred fully with the printers, &c. in this city, and are of opinion, that the proper types for printing the Bible are not to be had in this country, and that the paper cannot be procured, but with such difficulties and subject to such casualties, as render any dependence on it altogether improper: that to import types for the purpose of setting up an entire edition of the Bible, and to strike off 30,000 copies, with paper, binding, etc. will cost £10,272 10, which must be advanced by Congress, to be reimbursed by the sale of the books:

---

[23] *Letters of Delegates to Congress,* 7:311. At least one printer by July 10, 1777. *Letters of Delegates to Congress,* 7:312.

"That, your committee are of opinion, considerable difficulties will attend the procuring the types and paper; that, afterwards, the risk of importing them will considerably enhance the cost, and that the calculations are subject to such uncertainty in the present state of affairs, that Congress cannot much rely on them: that the use of the Bible is so universal, and its importance so great, that your committee refer the above to the consideration of Congress, and if Congress shall not think it expedient to order the importation of types and paper, your committee recommend that Congress will order the Committee of Commerce to import 20,000 Bibles from Holland, Scotland, or elsewhere, into the different ports of the states in the Union:"

Whereupon, the Congress was moved, to order the Committee of Commerce to import twenty thousand copies of the Bible.[24]

The final sentence in the above quotation is but one of thousands of pieces of evidence that refutes the contemporary secular and ahistorical interpretation of "separation of church and state." From the earliest formative movements of America's federal government, the Founding Fathers clearly demonstrated that Christianity would play an influential role in the development of the federal government, though it should not be accorded an institutional role.

It is important to note that the Continental Congress[25] voted to authorize the Committee of Commerce to purchase and import 20,000 Bibles. Despite the fact that the *Journals of Congress* records that permission was granted to purchase the Bibles, there was a difference of opinion between the states on the matter which may only be attributed to the

---

[24] *Journals of the Continental Congress,* 8:733-734.

[25] At this time, this was the Second Continental Congress.

fact that the delegates opposing the purchase acted merely under a financial consideration: "It could be nothing more than Congress's belief that it could not afford the project."[26] Throughout the War of Independence, resources of all types necessary to wage war against the British were dire, and though Congress believed the project to be very important, the three-member committee believed that to sponsor the printing of the Bible would be far too costly, and for this reason, purchasing it from sources that were more capable of producing the Bible was the suggested solution. As quoted above, Congress voted to purchase and distribute the Bible, which clearly demonstrates America's Founding Fathers never intended to remove American government from the influence of the teachings of the Bible!

Circumstances of war, however, prohibited Congress from completing the action that was sanctioned by the vote. The same day the Bible committee delivered its report and Congress approved the purchase of the Bibles was the day General Washington and his American troops lost the Battle of Brandywine Creek. As a result, British troops marched on Philadelphia, the capitol of the United States at that time, forcing the Continental Congress to abandon the city. Congress first moved to Lancaster, Pennsylvania for only a day and then to York, Pennsylvania. As a result, the decision to purchase and distribute 20,000 Bibles among the various states was never realized. The press of war took priority. Only a few years passed, however, before Congress once again took up the matter of acquiring Bibles for its citizenry, once again giving greater consideration to publishing Bibles in America.

Because of the pressures of war, three years passed before Congress once again addressed the matter. The fact that it did again arise demonstrates the collective concern shared by the members of Congress for this subject. That Congress addressed the question of purchasing and distributing the Bible at all completely denies the claim that America's Founding Fathers were secularists. On October 26, 1780, a

---

[26] Derek Davis, *Religion and the Continental Congress, 1774-1789: Contributions to Original Intent* (New York: Oxford University Press, 2000), 146.

simple resolution by James McLene kept this important subject before Congress:

> A motion was made by Mr. [James] McLene, seconded by Mr. [John] Hanson, respecting the printing of the Old and New Testament:
>
> Resolved, That it be recommended to such of the States who may think it convenient for them that they take proper measures to procure one or more new and correct editions of the old and new testament to be printed and that such states regulate their printers by law so as to secure effectually the said books from being misprinted.
>
> Ordered, That it be referred to a committee of three:
>
> The members chosen, Mr. [James] McLene, Mr. [Thomas] McKean and Mr. [James] Duane.[27]

The committee selected to oversee this resolution was to experience an alteration of one of its members and exercise a role in the printing of the only Bible ever authorized by Congress. Less than three months after this resolution was submitted to Congress, an important request was placed before Congress by one of the Philadelphia printers Congress had previously consulted concerning the feasibility of printing an edition of the Bible.

On January 21, 1781, well-known American printer, Robert Aitken,[28] sent a formal "memorial" or request to Congress for approval to print

---

[27] *Journals of the Continental Congress,* 18:979-980

[28] Robert Aitken had already secured impressive credentials as a printer. Among other works, he had been the publisher of the *Journals of Congress* for the first Congress (1774) and had published numerous articles by Thomas Paine, who would later be rejected by America's Founding Fathers for the irreligious influence the French Revolution would exercise over him. "The Bible of the

the first Bible in America. Only four years earlier, Congress had been advised that the resources to print the Bible were lacking in America, but now Robert Aitken possessed the printing resources and the will to print America's first English Bible—now known as the "Aitken Bible." He had been one of the Philadelphia printers the congressional committee had consulted in its first enquiry into printing the Bible in 1777, and now he presented Congress with his own request:

> To the Honorable The Congress
> of the United States of America
> The Memorial [Request] of Robert Aitken
> of the City of Philadelphia, Printer
>
> Humbly Showeth
>
> That in every well regulated government in Christendom the sacred books of the Old and New Testament, commonly called the Holy Bible, are printed and published under the authority of the sovereign powers, in order to prevent the fatal confusion that would arise, and the alarming injuries the Christian faith might suffer from the spurious and erroneous editions of Divine Revelation. That your memorialist[29][Robert Aitken] has no doubt but this work is an object worthy the attention of the Congress of the United States of America, who will not neglect spiritual security, while they are virtuously contending for temporal blessings. Under this persuasion your memorialist begs leave to, inform your Honors[30] that he both begun and made considerable progress in a neat edition of the Holy Scriptures for the use

---

American Revolution," *The Manhattan Rare Book Company* (http://www.theworldsgreatbooks.com/Aitken%20Bible.htm, November 20, 2013).

[29] Referring to the author himself—Robert Aitken.

[30] Referring to the members of the Continental Congress.

of schools, but being cautious of suffering his copy of the Bible to issue forth without the sanction of Congress, humbly prays that your Honors would take this important matter into serious consideration & would be pleased to appoint one member or members of your honorable body to inspect his work so that the same may be published under the authority of Congress. And further, your memorialist prays, that he may be commissioned or otherwise appointed & authorized to print and vend editions of, the Sacred Scriptures, in such manner and form as may best suit the wants and demands of the good people of these States, provided the same be in all things perfectly consonant to the Scriptures as heretofore established and received amongst us.[31]

After Robert Aitken presented his request to Congress, a small committee from Congress, composed of James Duane, Thomas McKean and Rev. Dr. John Witherspoon (President of Princeton), was appointed to collaborate with Aitken in his effort to print the Bible. From all appearances, this committee continued its work from about January of 1781 until September 1782.

This three-member committee from Congress, in turn, asked the two chaplains of Congress to examine the Bible on September 1, 1782. Less than two weeks before Congress' voted on the Aitken Bible, the two chaplains of Congress, Rev. Dr. William White of Christ Church (Episcopalian), Philadelphia, and Rev. George Duffield of the Third Presbyterian Church of Philadelphia, were requested to examine Aitken's work for accuracy. Rev. Jacob Duche had been the pastor of Christ Church and the first chaplain of the Congress and is often depicted in well-known works of art leading the First Congress in

---

[31] David Barton, "Aitken Bible," WallBuilders (http://www.wallbuilders. com/libissuesarticles.asp?id=46, November 20, 2013).

prayer. Rev. Duche deserted the American cause,[32] however, and was succeeded by Dr. White as pastor of Christ Church and successor as chaplain to the Congress. The practice of not allowing any single Christian denomination to dominate the religious interests of the federal government laid the foundation for the church-state relationship advocated by the First Amendment to the Constitution in 1789.

After the two chaplains of Congress had reviewed Aitken's Bible for accuracy, the three-man committee and the chaplains recommended that Congress endorse Robert Aitken's printing of the Bible. The *Journals of Congress* for Thursday, September 12, 1782 summarizes the details of the communications that began in January 1781 and concluded with the approval of Congress in September 1782.

William White

On the two pages following the title page of the Aitken Bible were printed the endorsements from Congress. The only difference between what was printed in the Aitken Bible and the *Journals of Congress* is the endorsement of the Secretary of Congress, Charles Thomson, placed at the very end of the quote.

[REPORT OF CONGRESSIONAL BIBLE COMMITTEE]

The committee, consisting of Mr. [James] Duane, Mr. [Thomas] McKean and Mr. [John] Witherspoon, to whom was referred a petition memorial [request] of Robert Aitken, printer, dated 21 January, 1781, respecting an edition of the Holy Scriptures, report,

That Mr. Aitken has at a great expense now finished an American edition of the Holy Scriptures in English;

---

[32] October 1, 1777.

that the committee have, from time to time, conferred with him attended to his progress in the work: that they also recommended it to the two chaplains of Congress to examine and give their opinion of the execution, who have accordingly reported thereon.

The recommendation and report being as follows:

Rev. Gentlemen, Our knowledge of your piety and public spirit leads us without apology to recommend to your particular attention the edition of the Holy Scriptures publishing by Mr. Aitken. He undertook this expensive work at a time, when from the circumstances of the war, an English edition of the Bible could not be imported, nor any opinion formed how long the obstruction might continue. On this account particularly he deserves applause and encouragement. We therefore wish you, reverend gentlemen, to examine the execution of the work, and if approved, to give it the sanction of your judgment and the weight of your recommendation.

We are with very great respect,
Your most obedient humble servants,

(Signed) James Duane, Chairman in behalf of a committee of Congress on Mr. Aitken's memorial.

[REPORT OF CHAPLAINS]

Rev. Dr. White and Rev. Mr. Duffield,

Chaplains of the United States in Congress assembled.

REPORT.

Gentlemen, Agreeably to your desire, we have paid attention to Mr. Robert Aitken's impression of the Holy Scriptures, of the old and new testament. Having selected and examined a variety of passages throughout the work, we are of opinion, that it is executed with great accuracy as to the sense, and with as few grammatical and typographical errors as could be expected in an undertaking of such magnitude. Being ourselves witnesses of the demand for this invaluable book, we rejoice in the present prospect of a supply, hoping that it will prove as advantageous as it is honorable to the gentleman, who has exerted himself to furnish it at the evident risk of private fortune. We are, gentlemen, your very respectful and humble servants,

(Signed) William White,
George Duffield.
Philadelphia, September 10, 1782.

Hon. James Duane, Esq. chairman, and the other hon. gentlemen of the committee of Congress on Mr. Aitken's memorial.

[Resolution of Congress to Approve the Aitken Bible]

Whereupon, Resolved, That the United States in Congress assembled, highly approve the pious and laudable undertaking of Mr. Aitken, as subservient to the interest of religion as well as an instance of the progress of arts in this country, and being satisfied from the above report, of his care and accuracy in the execution of the work, they recommend this edition of the Bible to the inhabitants of the United States, and

> hereby authorize him to publish this recommendation in the manner he shall think proper.
>
> Cha. Thomson, Sec'ry[33]

Although the Continental Congress provided no financial support for the printing of the Aitken Bible, the Pennsylvania legislature did advance Aitken $700 to complete the project.[34]

Following the resolution of the Congress to endorse Aitken's Bible (the last paragraph of the previous quote), the secretary of the Continental Congress, Charles Thomson, placed his name for additional verification, further involving and authenticating the action of Congress. Thomson had held the office of secretary of the Congress from the inception of the Continental Congress to the formation of the new government under the Constitution (1774-1789). In addition to his political contributions to America's independence, Thomson was well-known for his "Thompson Bible," the first American translation of the Greek Old Testament, as well as theological works such as *A Regular History of the Conception, Birth, Doctrine, Miracles, Death, Resurrection, and Ascension of Jesus Christ.* [35] Such were the Christian men and women who birthed America.

---

[33] *Journals of the Continental Congress,* 23:572-574. Compare with Davis, *Religion and the Continental Congress,* 146-147.

[34] Davis, *Religion and the Continental Congress,* 146.

[35] David Barton, "Aitken Bible," WallBuilders (http://www.wallbuilders. com/libissuesarticles.asp?id=46, November 20, 2013).

Three Founding
Fathers on the Bible

Those individuals who were most instrumental in the development of America as an independent nation are remembered as "Founding Fathers." Though America's legal foundation prior to the Revolutionary War was thoroughly Christian, important individuals who lived prior to the formation of our nation are not generally regarded as belonging to America's Founding Fathers. The expressions, "Fathers of America" or "Founding Fathers," is generally applied to the signers of the Declaration of Independence, those who labored and toiled in the Revolutionary War era, and those who helped to shape the Constitution and the post-Revolutionary War period. It is evident from a study of these periods and the individuals who dominated them that biblical Christian principles were driving forces in the formation of America. From among the numerous Founding Fathers, three individuals rose to greatest prominence: George Washington, Benjamin Franklin, and Dr. Benjamin Rush.[36] While the first two men have often been employed by secularists attempting to deny the Christian origin of America, Dr. Rush's Christian commitment was so evident from his biographical records that critics appear to have regarded the defamation of his Christian character useless. Despite secular attempts to besmirch President Washington and Dr. Franklin, all three of these men serve as a typical cross section of the overwhelming majority of America's

---

[36] John Sanderson, *Biography of the Signers to the Declaration of Independence* (Philadelphia: R.W. Pomeroy, 1823), 4:285.

Founding Fathers and for this reason are discussed below. A brief survey of the place the Bible (and its teachings) occupied in the lives of these three men should go a long way in refuting the argument of the irreligious that America was founded as a secular nation. Our brief survey of the influence of the Bible upon three of America's Founding Fathers must content itself with only a few of the most important examples of their advocacy of Christianity in general and the Bible in particular.

President George Washington

As a son of Virginia, George Washington was raised as an Anglican when Anglicanism was the state church of Virginia. Washington was raised in a Christian home,[37] received a Christian education,[38] was faithful in church attendance and worship of God,[39] respected the Sabbath principle by not working on Sunday,[40] was faithful in the habit of prayer,[41] financially supported

George Washington

his pastor,[42] signed the first Presidential Thanksgiving proclamation stating ". . . it is the duty of all nations to acknowledge the providence of Almighty God, to obey His will, to be grateful for His benefits . . .," and he began the tradition of taking the presidential oath of office with his right hand on the Bible—to mention only a few of the evidences of his Christian faith. Perhaps one of the best defenses of the Christian

---

[37] Peter Lillback, *George Washington's Sacred Fire* (Bryn Mawr Pa.: Providence Forum Press, 2006), 95ff.

[38] Lillback, *Washington's Sacred Fire*, 118.

[39] Morris, *Civil Institutions of the United States*, 498.

[40] Morris, *Civil Institutions of the United States*, 499.

[41] Morris, *Civil Institutions of the United States*, 500f.

[42] Lillback, *Washington's Sacred Fire*, 65.

faith and convictions of George Washington is presented in the massive volume, *George Washington's Sacred Fire*, written by Peter Lillback and Jerry Newcombe.[43] Readers wishing more detailed information into Mr. Washington's Christian commitment will be greatly benefitted by careful consultation of this work. This present summary will not attempt to parrot this monumental work of Lillback and Newcombe. As previously stated, the evidence supporting the fact that America was established as a Christian nation is voluminous, and just as the author must content himself with the presentation of some of the most salient historical evidences to support this point, so he must demonstrate restraint with regard to the biographical evidence that might also be produced.

A. Washington's General Orders

One of the ways that George Washington reflected his Christian faith and convictions is witnessed during America's War of Independence. On June 15, 1775, the American Continental Congress appointed one of its own members, George Washington, as Commander of the Continental Army. From the very beginning of his tenure in this office, it was evident that spiritual and religious matters were not issues of indifference to the new Commander. After making preparations to assume command, he finally did so more than two weeks later, on July 3. The "General Orders" delivered on July 3 were very brief, but the General Orders for the following day were more extensive and began to convey Washington's expectations for the deportment of the American army. In the third paragraph of the General Orders, the new Commander's spiritual expectations were first expressed:

> Head Quarters, Cambridge, July 4, 1775
>
> . . .
>
> The General most earnestly requires, and expects, a
> due observance of those articles of war, established

---

[43] Lillback, *Washington's Sacred Fire*. Also see, Edward McGuire, *The Religious Opinions and Character of Washington* (New York: Harper & Brothers, 1836).

for the Government of the army, which forbid profane cursing, swearing and drunkenness; And in like manner requires and expects, of all Officers, and Soldiers, not engaged on actual duty, a punctual attendance on divine Service, to implore the blessings of heaven upon the means used for our safety and defense.[44]

From the very beginning of his role as Commander of the Continental Army, Washington expected "all Officers, and Soldiers, not engaged on actual duty, a punctual attendance on divine Service, to implore the blessings of heaven upon the means used for our safety and defense." Not only did he advocate the Christian faith through the General Orders, but he also personally took an active role in leading worship. When a chaplain was not present to lead in "divine Service," General Washington personally read Scripture and prayed with his troops on Sundays.[45]

B. Circular Letter to States

One of Washington's most strident affirmations of his Christian convictions and the role that the Bible had exercised upon America was made in a circular letter at the end of the Revolution. This letter recognized a culmination of biblical influence—which historically, originated with King James' permission to settle the English holdings in the New World.

Prior to the organization of the Continental Congress in 1774, the American colonies did not concern themselves with the Christian observances in the other colonies. That is because that prior to the

---

[44] "The American Revolution, 1763-1783: Creating a Continental Army," *The Library of Congress* (http://www.loc.gov/teachers/classroommaterials/ presentationsandactivities/presentations/timeline/amrev/contarmy/orderone. html, November 12, 2015).

[45] Morris, *Civil Institutions of the United States*, 500f.

rise of the federal government—beginning with the Continental Congress—the American Colonies governed themselves, with oversight from the King and English Parliament. All charters and governments of the thirteen English colonies were Christian in character, reflecting the sentiments of the First Virginia Charter of King James I, which was signed on April 10, 1606, establishing the first permanent English settlement in the New World:

> We, greatly commending, and graciously accepting of, their desires for the furtherance of so noble a work, which may, by the Providence of Almighty God, hereafter tend to the glory of his Divine Majesty, in propagating of Christian religion to such people, as yet live in darkness and miserable ignorance of the true knowledge and worship of God, and may in time bring the infidels and savages, living in those parts, to human civility, and to a settled and quiet government: Do, by these our letters patents, graciously accept of, and agree to, their humble and well-intended desires.[46]

The Christian sentiment of King James was reflected in all the charters and constitutions of the thirteen American colonies, and when the Declaration of Independence was signed on July 4, 1776, the new constitutions of the states that soon followed continued to reflect their Christian origin. Nearly all of the original thirteen states had government-sponsored or supported churches.[47]

---

[46] "The First Charter of Virginia; April 10, 1606," Yale Law School, Lillian Goldman Law Library, accessed July 6, 2015. http://avalon.law.yale.edu/17th_century/va01.asp.

Orthography updated in quote.

[47] Eleven of the thirteen colonies/states originally had government sponsored Christian denominations. See Charles B. Galloway, *Christianity and the American Commonwealth: The Influence of Christianity in Making This Nation*, Reprint ed. (Powder Springs, Georgia: American Vision, 2005), 140.

Compare, Thomas Jefferson, *Notes on the State of Virginia*, A New Edition ed. (Richmond, VA: J. W. Randolph, 1853), 171-173.

John Jay

Mindful that the organization of the Continental Congress meant that representatives from these various government-sponsored denominational states were convening for the sake of governmental allegiance, these representatives were careful not to unnecessarily offend other Christian representatives from other states, lest the attempt at a unified government should fail. One of the most deeply committed evangelicals of the Founding Fathers, John Jay was America's first Chief Justice of the Supreme Court and, who at twenty-nine, was the youngest representative to the First Continental Congress. Jay was fearful that appointing a chaplain to Congress would heighten denominational differences prohibiting representatives from working together, but his fears were ill founded.[48] Seeking to dispel the myth that America's Founding Fathers were secularists, one author astutely perceived that Jay was not advancing a secular agenda:

> It would be a mistake to conclude from Jay's opposition to a chaplain in Congress that he was opposed to denominational religion. He was a consistent

---

[48] A note in the *Journals of Congress* explains those involved in the discussion concerning opening Congress with prayer: "'After settling the mode of voting, which is by giving each Colony an equal voice, it was agreed to open the business with prayer. As many of our warmest friends are members of the Church of England, [I] thought it prudent, as well on that as on some other accounts, to move that the service should be performed by a clergyman of that denomination' (Samuel Adams to J. Warren, 9 September, 1774). John Adams says it was Cushing who made the motion that business be opened with prayer, and John Jay and Rutledge opposed it on the ground of a diversity in religious sentiments. That Samuel Adams asserted he was no bigot, and could hear a prayer from any gentleman of piety and virtue, who was at the same time a friend to his country; and nominated Duché." *Journals of the Continental Congress, 1774-1789*, 34 vols. (Washington, D.C.: Government Printing Office, 1904), 1:26.

churchgoer and an opponent of Deism, particularly of the Thomas Paine variety.[49]

Anticipated denominational partisanship is the primary reason little mention was subsequently made of Christianity in America's most important national documents—Declaration of Independence, Articles of Confederation, Northwest Ordinance, and the United States Constitution, all of which make up America's "Organic Laws." However, this does not mean the representatives who ratified the four Organic Laws were in any stretch of the imagination "secular." Rather, they were respectful of fellow representatives who were of varying denominational and theological traditions. Because the individual states said a great deal about Christianity in their state laws and practices, it would have been difficult to find unanimity if the denominational and theological issues were insisted upon as the chief unifying influences. For this reason, religious matters were left to the individual states as reflected in the United States Constitution.

That General Washington was more than willing to be respectful of fellow Christians without divorcing himself from his Christian Anglican (or Episcopalian) tradition while exercising his official duties may be demonstrated from his writings. One particular occasion that reveals his belief that the Bible should be expected to influence matters of national government may be seen in a circular letter he penned near the end of his tenure as Commander of the American Revolutionary Army. On June 8, 1783, General Washington began to circulate a lengthy letter he had composed at his headquarters at Newburg, New York. Two months earlier, on April 11, 1783, word had reached Washington that a preliminary peace treaty had been signed between America and Great Britain to bring the American Revolution to a close. In his June 8 circular letter, he hoped to express his sentiments on some important issues, preparing America for a new phase of its life. Though copies of the letter were sent to the governors

[49] Norman Cousins, *"In God We Trust"; the Religious Beliefs and Ideas of the American Founding Fathers*, 1st ed. (New York: Harper, 1958), 360.

of the thirteen states, Washington intended that his sentiments should be more widely known beyond the governors themselves, saying he wished the governors would "communicate these sentiments to your Legislature at their next meeting, and that they may be considered as the legacy of one, who has ardently wished, on all occasions, to be useful to his Country."[50]

As he prepared to discuss the main points of his letter, he paused to praise the various influences that paved the way for America's optimistic future. But towering above all other influences that laid the "foundation" for America—the most important to General Washington—was "Revelation," or the Bible:

> The foundation of our Empire [America] was not laid in the gloomy age of ignorance and superstition, but at an epoch when the rights of mankind were better understood and more clearly defined, than at any former period, the researches of the human mind, after social happiness, have been carried to a great extent, the treasures of knowledge, acquired by the labors of philosophers, sages and legislatures, through a long succession of years, are laid open for our use, and their collected wisdom may be happily applied in the establishment of our forms of government; the free cultivation of letters, the unbounded extension of Commerce, the progressive refinement of manners, the growing liberality of sentiment, ***and above all, the pure and benign light of Revelation [the Bible]***, have had ameliorating influence on mankind and increased the blessings of society. At this auspicious period, the United States came into existence as a

---

[50] George Washington, "George Washington to Meshech Weare, Et Al, June 8, 1783, Circular Letter of Farewell to Army," Library of Congress, accessed January 2, 2016. http://memory.loc.gov/cgi-bin/query/r?ammem/mgw:@field%28DOCID+@lit%28gw260534%29%29.

nation, and if their citizens should not be completely free and happy, the fault will be entirely their own.[51]

Given the fact that deists did not believe "revelation" could occur and the irreligious believe it is unnecessary, it is not possible to interpret Washington's use of the term "Revelation" in any other way than what he would have been taught it meant as an Anglican—that is the revelation of God as recorded in the Bible! While Washington recognized other influences upon the "foundation of our Empire," the most important influence was not of human origin—something reflected in a study of the sources that most affected the Founding Fathers. In 1983, Charles S. Hyneman and Donald S. Lutz published the result of years of study in their two-volume work, *American Political Writing During the Founding Era, 1760-1805*.[52] After reviewing nearly 15,000 documents, the two professors concluded that, though many other sources of authority were cited in the writings of America's Founding Fathers, the single most quoted source of authority was the Bible. Though many of the Founding Fathers possessed classical educations and could read the classics of the Greco-Roman world in the original languages of Greek and Latin, the classical philosophers did not hold the greatest influence over their thinking. The above quote from General Washington recognizes other influences that gave rise to America, but—in his estimation—the single greatest influence for good upon the nation was "the pure and benign light of Revelation"— the Bible!

As he concluded his circular letter, the Commander of America's army continued to express his Christian faith in a form similar to that which may be attributed to any faithful minister of the Gospel:

> I now make it my earnest prayer, that God would have you, and the state over which you preside, in

---

[51] Washington, "Circular Letter of Farewell to Army."
[52] Charles S. Hyneman and Donald S. Lutz, *American Political Writing During the Founding Era, 1760-1805*, 2 vols. (Indianapolis: Liberty Press, 1983).

his holy protection, that he would incline the hearts of the citizens to cultivate a spirit of subordination and obedience to government, to entertain a brotherly affection and love for one another, for their fellow citizens of the United States at large, and particularly for their brethren who have served in the field, and finally, that he would most graciously be pleased to dispose us all, to do justice, to love mercy, and to demean ourselves with that charity, humility and pacific [or peaceable] temper of mind, which were the characteristics of the Divine Author of our blessed [Christian] religion, and without an humble imitation of whose example in these things, we can never hope to be a happy nation.[53]

A benediction completely unsuited to a secularist, atheist, agnostic, deist, or any other form of irreligion!

C. Fidelity in Private Spiritual Habits

Biographical evidence suggests George Washington was an advocate of Christianity, not only in public, but in his private life as well. Many years after his death, an important spiritual habit of Washington was recounted and added to what was already known concerning his Christian devotional habits. From all indication, the account recorded below reflects a habit that characterized Mr. Washington's entire life— though it likely varied to some degree because of the circumstances of life.[54] In a letter written on January 10, 1859, Nathaniel Hewit recalled

---

[53] Washington, "Circular Letter of Farewell to Army."

[54] One of the most widely circulated biographies of George Washington was a small volume published by the American Sunday School Union. This work recounted what was reported concerning the prayer or devotional life of Washington in the war years by a variety of sources. Anna C. Reed, *Life of Washington* (n.p.: American Sunday-School Union, 1824; reprint, Green Forest: AR, Attic Books, 2010), 117-19.

an experience that occurred nearly thirty years earlier that recounted Washington's faithful Christian devotional habits.

> In the month of November, 1829, I was in Fredericksburg, Va., and in the family of the Rev. Mr. Wilson, pastor of the Presbyterian church in that place. He occupied the house in which the mother of Washington lived and died. Mr. Wilson informed me that a nephew of Washington, Captain Lewis, who had been his clerk, and had the charge of his books and papers, and was daily in his library until his decease, related to him the following occurrence. It was the custom of Washington to retire to his library every evening precisely at nine o'clock, and, although he had visitors, he invariably left at that hour, and did not return. He remained alone in his library till ten o'clock, and passed into his bedchamber by an inner door. Captain Lewis had long wondered how he spent that hour, knowing that he wrote nothing, and that the books and papers were as he himself left them the preceding day. During a violent storm of wind and rain, and when there were no visitors, he crept in his stocking-feet to the door, and through the key-hole he beheld him on his knees, with a large book open before him, which he had no doubt was a Bible—a large one being constantly in the room.[55]

This observation of his devotional life was confirmed by Washington's adopted daughter. Early in the twentieth century, America and Her Founding Fathers came under the attack of secular socialistic forces that had swept through Europe and was advancing to other venues around the globe. The person and character of George Washington was not spared from this withering attack of irreligious secularists, which continues now into the early portion of the twenty-first century in the

---

[55] Morris, *Civil Institutions of the United States*, 501-502.

form of historical revisionism. Attempting to renounce or recast the character of Washington and other Founding Fathers, these secularists completely reject the most important biographical and historical records in favor of any information—no matter how tenuous—that will debunk well-established truth that often recounts the Christian influence that birthed America. The fact is that the Founding Fathers bequeathed much biographical information concerning their Christian spiritual commitments.

When George Washington married the young widow, Martha Custis, two young children (John and Martha, also called Patsy) were brought into his home from Martha's previous marriage. Upon maturity, both John and Martha Patsy married and had children of their own, but tragedy struck both children, and by 1781, both John and Martha Patsy were dead.

John left four young children behind, ranging in age from infancy to six years. Occupied with the duties of the Commander of the American revolutionary army, George Washington unsuccessfully attempted to convince Martha's brother to raise the children. Unable to raise all four children, John's widow allowed George and Martha to adopt the two younger children—Nelly Parke Custis and George Washington Parke Custis.

Nelly lived with her grandparents as their adopted daughter for twenty years, nearly from her birth in 1779 to 1799, the year of her marriage, and referred to George and Martha as her "beloved parents." It is not surprising, then, for Washington's biographer to write to Nelly, asking her for biographical insight concerning Mr. Washington's faith. On February 26, 1833, she responded to the enquiry of biographer Jared Sparks, a portion of which reflected specifically upon Washington's personal devotional habits:

> It was his custom to retire to his library at nine or ten
> o'clock, where he remained an hour before he went

to his chamber. He always rose before the sun, and remained in his library until called to breakfast. I never witnessed his private devotions. I never inquired about them. I should have thought it the greatest heresy to doubt his firm belief in Christianity. His life, his writings, prove that he was a Christian. He was not one of those, who act or pray, 'that they may be seen of men.' He communed with his God in secret.

My mother resided two years at Mount Vernon, after her marriage with John Parke Custis, the only son of Mrs. Washington. I have heard her say, that General Washington always received the sacrament with my grandmother before the revolution. When my aunt, Miss Custis, died suddenly at Mount Vernon, before they could realize the event, he knelt by her and prayed most fervently, most affectingly, for her recovery. Of this I was assured by Judge Washington's mother, and other witnesses.[56]

In the same letter, Nelly also recounted Martha Washington's devotional fidelity and the perceived influence that this spiritual state had upon the couple:

She never omitted her private devotions, or her public duties; and she and her husband were so perfectly united and happy, that he must have been a Christian. She had no doubts, no fears for him. After forty years of devoted affection and uninterrupted happiness, she resigned him without a murmur into the arms of his

---

[56] Jared Sparks, *The Writings of George Washington; Being His Correspondence, Addresses, Messages, and Other Papers, Official and Private, Selected and Published from the Original Manuscripts; with a Life of the Author, Notes, and Illustrations,* 12 vols. (Boston: Little, Brown, 1858), 12:406.

> Saviour and his God, with the assured hope of his
> eternal felicity.[57]

That Washington maintained a private devotional life during the busy days of his tenure as Commander of the Continental Army was recounted for generations of Americans in a biography of Washington published by the American Sunday School Union (ASSU—discussed further below). Used as a means of promoting the biblical principles that gave rise to America, Founding Fathers sought to use the ASSU to ensure succeeding generations of Americans would perpetuate the American Republic with the Christian principles that had established it, and the libraries of Christian materials the ASSU produced was an important part of that effort. In some communities, these small libraries were the largest literary repositories in the area. Among some of the first books to be printed was a biography of George Washington, written by Anna C. Reed. In it, the personal, moral, and spiritual life of the Father of America was related to young readers, challenging them to follow in the footsteps of this great American. Anna Reed related one of the most vivid stories of General Washington's spiritual life that occurred when the General and his troops were in winter quarters in Valley Forge, which extended from December 19, 1777 to June 19, 1778. Various artists have attempted to capture this scene with their brushes. After describing in some detail the hardships under which the American troops lived at Valley Forge, Reed proceeded to relate the following anecdote of General Washington's prayer life. She began with a quote from a letter the General was writing to Patrick Henry concerning the hardships of the soldiers. General Washington was surprised that the soldiers did not lament the conditions at Valley Forge. Reed wrote,

> In describing their condition in the hut-camp, he
> said [in his letter to Patrick Henry, then governor
> of Virginia], "For some days there has been little less
> than a famine in the camp; but, naked and starving

---

as they are, I cannot enough admire the incomparable fidelity of the soldiers, that they have not before this time been excited to a general mutiny or dispersion."

The inhabitants of the surrounding country, knowing this sad state of the army, were very uneasy; one of them left his home, one day, and as he was passing thoughtfully the edge of a wood near the hut-camp, he heard low sounds of a voice. He stopped to listen, and looking between the trunks of the large trees he saw Gen. Washington engaged in prayer. He passed quietly on, that he might not disturb him; and, on returning home, told this family he knew the Americans would succeed, for their leader did not trust in his own strength, but sought aid from the hearer of prayer, who promised in his word, "Call upon me in the day of trouble; I will deliver thee, and thou shalt glorify me." A female, who lived at the Valley Forge when the army was encamped there, told a friend who visited her soon after they left it, that she had discovered that it was the habit of Washington to retire to a short distance from the camp to worship God in prayer. Many, who in "the day of prosperity" have forgotten or neglected to worship their Creator, will earnestly call upon him in " the day of trouble," when they feel that His power only can deliver them; but it was not thus with Washington; it was his constant custom as one of his nephews has thus related: "One morning, at daybreak, an officer came to the general's quarters with dispatches. As such communications usually passed through my hands, I took the papers from the messenger and directed my steps towards the general's room. Walking along the passage which led to his door, I heard a voice within. I paused, and distinctly recognized the voice of the general. Listening for a moment, when all was silent around, I found that he was earnestly engaged in prayer. *I knew this to be his habit*, and therefore retired, with the papers in my hand, till such time as I supposed he had finished the exercise, when I returned, knocked at his door, and was admitted." Thus, in obedience to Him whom he called " the Divine Author of our blessed religion," Washington, in the retirement of his chamber, prayed to his "Father who seeth in secret," and truly his "Father, who seeth in secret," did " reward him openly."[58]

D. The Bible in Death

While much more might be presented to demonstrate the importance of the Christian religion and the role of the Bible in the life of George Washington, perhaps the evidence of his faith at the moment of death is most compelling. There is no evidence that George Washington was ashamed of his Christian faith; rather, just the opposite was true. Throughout his life he conducted himself as a Christian—

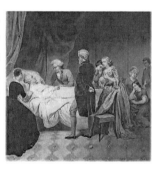

Death of George Washington

even the scene of his deathbed reflected the Christian commitment that characterized his life. On December 14, 1799—at the age of sixty-eight—President Washington passed from this world, the scene of which was captured by one of his biographers—the place of Scripture and its teachings accompanying him to the "valley of the shadow of death":

> His death was worthy of his Christian faith and character. "I die hard," said he; "but I am not afraid

---

[58] Anna C. Reed, *Life of Washington* (n.p.: American Sunday-School Union, 1824; reprint, Green Forest: AR, Attic Books, 2010), 117-19.

to die. I should have been glad, had it pleased God, to die a little easier; but I doubt not it is for my good. 'Tis well! Father of mercies, take me to thyself." On his dying bed lay an open Bible, the book of God, which he had read in the family circle and in his private devotions, and in the light of its heavenly truths his great soul passed, doubtless, into the light and immortality of heaven.[59]

In responding to those who doubted George Washington's Christian commitment, one of his most astute biographers, answered their doubt with a rhetorical question, "... is it credible, that, in a matter of the highest and most serious importance [Washington's faith], he should practice through a long series of years, a deliberate deception upon his friends and the public? It is neither credible nor possible."[60] In short, Washington died as he had sought to live—in the embrace of the Christian religion.

Benjamin Franklin

Of all of America's Founding Fathers, Benjamin Franklin and Thomas Jefferson possessed the most unorthodox Christian theology. However, their understanding of Christianity was far more orthodox than many contemporary "Christians." Neither Franklin nor Jefferson were deists, atheists, agnostics, or irreligious in any sense. Secularists who seek to deny Americans their Christian heritage have no patrons to whom they may turn for support among America's

Benjamin Franklin

---

[59] Morris, *Civil Institutions of the United States*, 520.
[60] Sparks, 12:405.

Founding Fathers—absolutely none![61] For this reason, they seek to employ Franklin and Jefferson to do their secular and irreligious bidding.

Benjamin Franklin was raised in a Christian home, his father, Josiah, having descended from Puritans. Franklin was born on January 17, 1706 and soon after baptized at well known Old South Meeting House in Boston, Massachusetts. Josiah and Abiah Franklin wished that their son Benjamin should become a minister of the gospel, and they began to educate him with that goal in mind, but their meager resources could not adequately supply for his preparation for the ministry, so their goal was eventually abandoned. Deserting an apprenticeship with his brother, Benjamin fled to Philadelphia, Pennsylvania where he began to invest his life's energies. Before recounting advocacy of Christianity as one of America's Founding Fathers, knowledge of an important era of his life is critical to a proper understanding of Franklin's thoughts concerning religion.

A. The Influence of Infidelity upon Franklin

In a letter to a friend in New Castle, Delaware, Benjamin Franklin graphically described the journey of his youth from Boston to Philadelphia—when fleeing from the apprenticeship with his brother. A copy of this letter made its way into the hands of the Governor of Pennsylvania,

Benjamin Franklin Works On Printing Press

---

[61] Given the fact that Thomas Paine based his book *Common Sense* upon the Bible, it is not possible to refer to Paine as a secularist at the point he wrote and published this book. Only after Paine traveled to France and participated in the irreligious blood-letting French Revolution did he advocate secularism in his books *Rights of Man* (1791) and *Age of Reason* (1793-1794). Upon espousing his secularism following his return to America, Paine was rejected by the Founding Fathers because of his irreligion.

Sir William Keith, who invited young Benjamin to his mansion. A friendship arose from their first meeting, with the Governor encouraging and offering his support to Ben to establish his own business. The proposed business plan was extensive, and involved a voyage to England for materials.

Franklin made the trip, arrived in London, but to his dismay, found the promised support of Sir William Keith of little or no avail. Forced to provide for himself, Ben obtained employment as a journeyman printer in one of the important businesses in the city. Here his industry, studious spirit, punctuality, and frugality, soon won him a number of friends. To his detriment, he soon came under the influence of some irreligious infidels, among whom was Lord Mandeville. Though Ben had come under the influence of deism as early as age fifteen, he experienced first hand the abusiveness that such philosophy produces and had come to believe this doctrine produced pernicious character and was "not very useful".[62] Under the influence of these infidels, his mind was quickly tainted with irreligious infidelity, which he published in the form of a pamphlet. Later in life, however, he regretted having written this pamphlet and candidly condemned his immature musings. Though he lamented the content of this pamphlet, the influence of Lord Mandeville and his fellow infidels changed Franklin's views concerning Jesus Christ—but that Franklin quickly forsook his brief flirtation with deism is evident from his emphasis upon God's providence or God's continuing work in the world.[63]

---

[62] Benjamin Franklin, *The Autobiography of Benjamin Franklin with Notes and a Sketch of Franklin's Life from the Point Where the Autobiography Ends, Drawn Chiefly from His Letters* (Boston: Houghton, Mifflin and Company, 1888), 78.

[63] See Franklin's discussion of God's work in the world in his lecture, "A Lecture on The Providence of God in The Government The World," in Morris, *Civil Institutions of the United States*, 131-134.

B. The Bible and Pennsylvania's First Constitution

That Franklin recognized the importance of the role of Christianity in government may be demonstrated by his role in the composition of Pennsylvania's first constitution. In 1776, Franklin was appointed to the Committee of Five[64] to draft a Declaration of Independence from King George III and the British Isles; he voted for its adoption, and signed it with most of the other delegates on the second of August. Soon after this, a

Declaration of Independence (Committee of Five)

convention was called in Pennsylvania for the purpose of organizing the state government in accordance with the recommendation of the Continental Congress. He was chosen President of Pennsylvania's Constitutional Convention, and his wisdom was manifested in what was produced by the convention. Again, the Christian convictions of Franklin and the other delegates that helped prepare Pennsylvania's first constitution were plainly engrafted into the text. Consistent with the patents, charters, and legal foundations of all Thirteen Colonies prior to the American Revolution, Pennsylvania's constitution reflected its Christian origin. On September 28, 1776, Franklin—as president of the convention—signed Pennsylvania's first constitution, Section 10, which legislated a Christian test for all who would occupy a seat in Pennsylvania's assembly:

> And each member, before he takes his seat, shall make and subscribe the following declaration, ... [namely]: 'I do believe in one God, the Creator and Governor of the Universe, the Rewarder of the good and the Punisher of the wicked. And I do acknowledge the

---

[64] The Committee of Five was composed of John Adams of Massachusetts, Benjamin Franklin of Pennsylvania, Thomas Jefferson of Virginia, Robert R. Livingston of New York, and Roger Sherman of Connecticut.

Scriptures of the Old and New Testament to be given by Divine Inspiration. And no further or other religious test shall ever hereafter be required of any civil officer or magistrate in this State.'[65]

The expectations of this portion of Pennsylvania's constitution ensured that only professing Christians—or those who held to these important Christian doctrines—could expect to hold a seat in Pennsylvania's state legislature. Unfortunately, to acknowledge "the Scriptures of the Old and New Testament to be given by Divine Inspiration" is more than many pastors and professors at Christian institutions are willing to profess in the present generation. Because other newly developed state constitutions had similar doctrinal statements and standards, the Founding Fathers were far more "Christian" than many professing the faith today.

Contrary to what secularists in America now argue, Franklin saw little influence of unbelief in its various secular manifestations in his day; rather, he saw the flourishing of various Christian denominations. In 1782, he developed a brief description of what those who anticipated moving to America could expect to find there. In his description of America's religious life and God's providence in the life of the nation, he wrote:

> . . . bad examples to youth are more rare in America, which must be a comfortable consideration to parents. To this may be truly added, that serious religion, under its various denominations, is not only tolerated, but respected and practiced. Atheism is unknown there; infidelity [deism] rare and secret; so that persons may live to a great age in that country, without having their piety [Christian scruples] shocked by meeting with either an atheist or an infidel. And the Divine Being seems to have manifested his approbation of

---

[65] "American Minute with Bill Federer," April 17, 2015.

the mutual forbearance and kindness with which the different Sects [Christian denominations] treat each other, by the remarkable prosperity with which He has been pleased to favor the whole country.[66]

C. Franklin Rejects Paine's Infidelity

If it may be shown that Benjamin Franklin resisted irreligious secularism and did what was in his power to dissuade and reject such efforts, then—since Franklin was comparatively less orthodox in his Christian beliefs than other Founding Fathers—it is reasonable to believe that other Founding Fathers who were more traditional than Franklin would be more eager to advocate the influence of

Thomas Paine

Christianity. And in fact, Mr. Franklin has provided us with such evidence.

Thomas Pain had commended himself to the American patriots with the anonymously published work, *Common Sense*, on January 10, 1776. He had composed *Common Sense* in a style readily understood by the average American colonist. In fact, Paine structured *Common Sense* as if it were a sermon and relied upon biblical references to help argue his case. He initially intended to name the work *Plain Truth* but his good friend, Dr. Benjamin Rush, was responsible for the title under which the work commended itself to the American Colonies.

Paine left America following the Revolution, returning first to England before traveling to France in 1790 to witness the French Revolution first-hand. Here, he was imbued with the irreligious

---

[66] "Benjamin Franklin, Information to Those Who Would Remove to America," *The Founders' Constitution* (http://press-pubs.uchicago.edu/founders/documents/v1ch15s27.html, April 17, 2015).

infidelity of Voltaire, Rousseau, and other French "Intellectuals." It was this influence that gave rise to Paine's most irreligious writings. In 1794, Thomas Paine published his infamous work, *Age of Reason*, in which he elevated "free thought" and the principles of deism while he attacked Christianity and the providence of God in the world— something Franklin and the American Founding Fathers vigorously rejected.

Paine had sent a manuscript copy of this work to Mr. Franklin before Franklin's death. After reading it, Mr. Franklin responded, urging him not to publish it. As he closed his letter to Paine, Franklin wrote,

> …think how great a portion of mankind consists of weak and ignorant men and women, and of inexperienced, inconsiderate youth of both sexes, who have need of the motives of [the Christian] religion to restrain them from vice, to support their virtue, and retain them in the practice of it till it becomes habitual, which is the great point for its security. And perhaps you are indebted to her originally, that is, to your religious education [of your youth], for the habits of virtue upon which you now justly value yourself. You might easily display your excellent talents of reasoning upon a less hazardous subject, and thereby obtain a rank with our most distinguished authors. For among us it is not necessary, as among the Hottentots, that a youth, to be raised into the company of men, should prove his manhood by beating his mother.
>
> I would advise you, therefore, not to attempt unchaining the tiger [or publish this work], but to burn this piece before it is seen by any other

person; whereby you will save yourself a great deal of
mortification by the enemies it may raise against you,
and perhaps a good deal of regret and repentance. If
men are so wicked with religion, what would they be
if without it. I intend this letter itself as a proof of my
friendship, and therefore add no professions to it; but
subscribe simply yours,

B. Franklin[67]

Though influenced as early as his mid-teens by deism, infidelity, and
irreligion, Benjamin Franklin had come to realize it only produced
heartache and misery.[68] In world history, where have agnosticism,
atheism, deism, and other forms of irreligion produced wellbeing and
a truly progressive society? Nowhere!

Far from attempting to publically marginalize the Bible and the
Christian faith, Franklin—like all of America's Founding Fathers—
believed the Bible and Christianity which arises from it must be
publically expressed and observed. One of Franklin's sayings reveals
that he believed the Bible produced the genius that provides stability
and progress to free governments and to the diffusion of liberty:

> A Bible and a newspaper in every house, a good school
> in every district, all studied and appreciated as they
> merit, are the principal supports of virtue, morality,
> and civil liberty.[69]

[67] Jared Sparks, *The Works of Benjamin Franklin*, (Boston: Tappan, Whittemore, and Mason, 1840), 10:281-282; quoted in "Benjamin Franklin's letter to Thomas Paine," *WallBuilders* (http://www.wallbuilders.com/libissuesarticles. asp?id=58, April 15, 2015).

[68] Franklin, 77-78.

[69] Morris, *Civil Institutions of the United States*, 134.

Dr. Benjamin Rush

The third most influential Founding
Father in the era following the American
Revolution was Dr. Benjamin Rush of
Philadelphia, Pennsylvania. He is known
as the "Father of American Medicine,"[70]
and "The Father of Public Schools
Under the Constitution."[71] Like the
overwhelming majority of the signers of
the Declaration of Independence, Dr.
Rush was opposed to slavery. As one of the
first organizers of America's first anti-slavery society[72] he soon became
a leader in the national abolition movement, which was primarily led
by Christians.[73]

Benjamin Rush

Benjamin, the fourth child of the family, was born on January 4,
1746,[74] at Berberry, about twelve miles northeast of Philadelphia. When

---

[70] Thomas Mitchell, *The Character of Rush: An Introductory to the Course
on the Theory and Practice of Medicine, in the Philadelphia College of Medicine*
(Philadelphia [Pa.]: John H. Gihon Printer, 1848), 4.

[71] David Ramsay, *An Eulogium Upon Benjamin Rush, M.D., Professor of
the Institutes and Practice of Medicine and of Clinical Practice in the University of
Pennsylvania. Who Departed This Life April 19, 1813, in the Sixty-Ninth Year of His
Age. Written at the Request of the Medical Society of South Carolina, and Delivered
before Them and Others, in the Circular Church of Charleston, on the 10ᵗʰ of June,
1813, and Pub. At Their Request* (Phildelphia: Bradford and Inskeep, 1813), 107.

[72] Dr. Rush was listed as one of two secretaries of the society. See Pennsylvania
Society for Promoting the Abolition of Slavery, *Centennial Anniversary of the
Pennsylvania Society, for Promoting the Abolition of Slavery, the Relief of Free Negroes
Unlawfully Held in Bondage: And for Improving the Condition of the African Race*
(Philadelphia: Grant, Faires & Rodgers, printers, 1875), 7.

[73] Pennsylvania Society for Promoting the Abolition of Slavery, 14-15.
Also see, "Dr. Benjamin Rush," WallBuilders (http://www.wallbuilders.com/
libissuesarticles.asp?id=147218, April 21, 2015).

[74] Older dating places his birth on December 24, 1745. To Benjamin's
parents, John Harvey Rush and Susanna Hall Rush, were born seven children.

Benjamin was only six years old, his father died, leaving the care of the family in the hands of his mother, Susanna. Believing her small farm would not provide for the education of her children, Susanna sold her land and moved to Philadelphia, where she began a commercial endeavor—which was very likely a small store.[75] By the time Benjamin was nine, his mother had been sufficiently successful to secure a place for him in the West Nottingham Academy, which was under the direction of its founder, Rev. Dr. Samuel Finley, whose wife, Sarah, was Benjamin's aunt, the sister of Benjamin's mother.

A. His Biblical Education at Princeton

To absolve Benjamin Rush of the label of "leader of the American Enlightenment"[76] that liberals have placed upon him, more must be understood about the remarkable evangelical Christian environment in which he was educated—an environment that not only helped to shape his life but also shaped the life of America. His uncle and schoolmaster, Rev. Dr. Samuel Finley, was educated in William Tennent's Log

John Witherspoon

College, in Neshaminy, Bucks County, Pennsylvania—a forerunner of present-day Princeton University. In 1761, Dr. Finley became the president of Princeton, holding that position until his untimely death on July 17, 1766. William Tennent and Samuel Finley were part of the evangelical Calvinistic Presbyterian tradition that was so instrumental in shaping America into an independent nation. In fact, another president of Princeton, Rev. Dr. John Witherspoon, was also a signer of the Declaration of Independence. For those seeking to rewrite American history with the secular appeal to the "American

---

[75] John Sanderson, *Biography of the Signers to the Declaration of Independence*, 4 vols. (Philadelphia: R. W. Pomeroy, 1823), 4:250-51.

[76] "Benjamin Rush," *Wikipedia* (http://en.wikipedia.org/wiki/Benjamin_Rush, April 29, 2015).

Enlightenment," they are uninformed when they seek to apply this expression to the Founding Fathers—above all when they seek to apply it to Dr. Rush, who was one of the most deeply dedicated evangelical leaders of the American Revolution. But more importantly, they were leaders in the first Great Awakening that helped to lay the spiritual foundation for America's national independence.

After studying with his Uncle at his West Nottingham Academy, Benjamin was accepted in 1758 into studies at Princeton College—at the age of fourteen. At that time, Princeton was under the presidency of the former orator and pastor of Patrick Henry, Rev. Dr. Samuel Davies. The oratorical skill and success of that great American statesman, Patrick Henry, is due in large part to the fact that he sat under the preaching ministry of Rev. Davies. The influence of such Christian extraordinary ministers of the Gospel shaped the foundation of America through the influence they exercised over their spiritual descendants, such as Patrick Henry and Benjamin Rush. One of Benjamin Rush's biographers accurately judged the influence of these spiritual giants upon his life when he wrote the following:

> Such was the force of the example and pious principles, which he received at this time, . . . that though he spent nearly all the remainder of his youth in Edinburgh, London, and Paris, exposed to every temptation inseparable from such great cities, yet he returned at the age of twenty-four years to his native county, with the same innocence of morals, which he brought with him from Nottingham, the scene of his boyish years.[77]

Two years after entering Princeton, Benjamin graduated with a Bachelor of Arts degree—in 1760 at the age of sixteen. Like many other American Founding Fathers, Benjamin excelled in academics. One writer called attention to this aptitude when he wrote that Benjamin was "said to

---

[77] Sanderson, 4:251-52.

have advanced in learning far beyond the ordinary proficiency of his age, and to have acquired that love of order and emulation of study, which distinguished him throughout the . . . [remainder] of his life.[78]

Though initially inclined to study law, his Uncle, Dr. Finley, is believed to have encouraged him to take up the study of medicine and placed him under the direction of Doctor John Redman of Philadelphia who helped to oversee his studies for this undertaking. From 1761 to 1766, Benjamin apprenticed under Dr. Redman.

With the encouragement of Dr. Redman, Benjamin continued his studies at the University of Edinburgh in Scotland, studying there from 1766 to 1768 and earned the degree of "Doctor of Medicine".[79] While living in Edinburgh, Benjamin was requested by the trustees to offer once again the presidency of Princeton to Dr. John Witherspoon, who at that time was ministering in Paisley, Scotland. Reversing his decision to decline this office, Dr. Witherspoon was persuaded by Benjamin to accept the invitation. Only a few years would pass before both men would subscribe their names on the Declaration of Independence. Before returning home to the American Colonies, he toured Europe, having become fluent in French, Italian, and Spanish. In the autumn of 1769, he returned home, established a medical practice in Philadelphia, and was appointed Professor of Chemistry at the College of Philadelphia (now the University of Pennsylvania).

B. Influence Before and After Revolution

Doctor Rush took up the cause of American patriotism immediately after his return to America following his studies at Edinburgh in 1769, and his pen proved to be a powerful instrument in arousing the people

---

[78] Sanderson, 4:251.

[79] His thesis was, *de coctione ciborium*, which was both presented and defended in Latin. Sanderson, 4:254.

to action. He became active in the Sons of Liberty[80] and was invited to take a seat in the Continental Congress of 1775, but declined at that time; but when some of the Pennsylvania delegates to the Continental Congress refused to vote for Independence and withdrew from their seats the following year, he was elected to fill one of them, and this time did not hesitate to accept it. Rush's name appears on the Declaration of Independence to the right of John Hancock's signature and immediately above Benjamin Franklin's.

Signing of Declaration of Independence

Following the Revolution, his public service was more limited; in fact, with the exception of being a member of the Convention of Pennsylvania, which adopted the Federal Constitution on December 12, 1787,[81] he did not actively participate in any public duties, with one exception. In 1788, he was appointed treasurer of the United States Mint, serving from 1797 to 1813.

C. Becomes Leading Biblical Advocate

As a Christian, Dr. Rush was zealous and consistent in the observance of Christian disciplines. Throughout his life, the Bible was a "lamp to his feet,"—his guide in all

John Wesley

things concerning his duty toward God and man. In the midst of all his diligent pursuit of human knowledge, he did not neglect searching the Scriptures for that knowledge that correctly directs the soul in its

---

[80] "Benjamin Rush," *Wikipedia* (http://en.wikipedia.org/wiki/Benjamin_Rush, May 2, 2015).

[81] Pennsylvania ratified the United States Constitution on December 12, 1787: 46 votes for; 23 against it.

journey to another world. His belief in the revelation of the Bible and the divine inspiration of the Sacred Writers is evident in his scientific writings. During that period at the end of the eighteenth century when the sentiments of French infidelity[82] were readily accepted by men in high places, Dr. Rush's principles stood firm and his opinions never wavered.[83]

Methodism, founded by John Wesley, eventually laid claim to Dr. Rush's most mature religious sentiments. Though it is known that Dr. Rush visited a variety of Christian denominational churches demonstrating a fraternal interest in them, he confessed that he surrendered his Calvinistic theology in favor of the Arminian teachings of Methodism. It was the Methodist writings of John William Fletcher, pastor of Madeley parish in England, that became most persuasive to him.[84] The Methodist leadership knew Dr. Rush. Henry Boehm, the traveling companion of well-known Methodist bishop, Francis Asbury, quoted from Asbury's *Journal* concerning one occasion when Dr. Rush paid the Bishop a visit. Boehm quoted Asbury, saying,

> I preached in Germantown [Pennsylvania]. Drs. Rush and Physic paid me a visit. How consoling it is to know that these great characters are men fearing God! I was much gratified, as I ever am, by their attentions, kindness, and charming conversation; indeed they have been of eminent use to me, and I acknowledge their services with gratitude.[85]

---

[82] Though the French assisted America in its fight for freedom, the infidelity and irreligion that was popularized by Voltaire, Jean Jacques Rousseau, and the Intellectuals also accompanied French soldiers to America and remained long after the Revolution.

[83] B. J. Lossing, *Signers of the Declaration of Independence* (New York: Geo. F. Cooledge, 1848), 103.

[84] "Benjamin Rush," *Wikipedia* (http://en.wikipedia.org/wiki/Benjamin_Rush, May 1, 2015).

[85] Henry Boehm, *The Patriarch of One Hundred Years Being Reminiscences, Historical and Biographical, of Rev. Henry Boehm*, 1982 reprint ed. (New York:

Among Rush's favorite Methodist preachers was Harry Hoosier, better known as "Black Harry,"[86] who appears to have gained his freedom from slavery following the American Revolution. Harry Hoosier's influence was so extensive that many of his followers—especially those opposed to slavery—became known as "Hoosiers," especially in the state of Indiana.[87] It is a little-known fact that the "Hoosiers" of Indiana may thank a black Methodist preacher for their nickname. Dr. Rush said that, "making allowances for his illiteracy, [Harry Hoosier] . . . was the greatest orator in America".[88]

Dr. Rush was instrumental in the formation and development of two important American spiritual institutions—Bible Societies and the Sunday School. Many of America's Founding Fathers became members of Bible societies, and Dr. Rush was a founding member of America's first Bible Society, which was the Pennsylvania Bible Society.[89] The first formal meeting of the Society was convened on December 12, 1808. The chaplain of the United States Congress, Rev. Dr. William White, was elected president, and Dr. Rush was elected vice-president. Less than a decade later, a national effort was made to organize a Bible society to distribute Scripture. As will be noticed in the pages that follow, the American Bible Society was then founded by one of the presidents of America's Continental Congress.

Nelson & Phillips, 1875), 343.

[86] Boehm, 90-92.

[87] Fisk University Professor William D. Piersen makes this argument. "Harry Hoosier," *Moment in Indiana History* (http://indianapublicmedia.org/momentofindianahistory/harry-hoosier/, November 17, 2015).

[88] Stephen H. Webb, "Introducing Black Harry Hoosier: The History Behind Indiana's Namesake," *Indiana Magazine of History*, Vol. XCVIII (March 2002); "Harry Hoosier," *Wikipedia* (http://en.wikipedia.org/wiki/Harry_Hoosier#cite_note-intro-2, May 1, 2015).

[89] *The First Report of the Bible Society, Established in Philadelphia Read before the Society at Their Annual Meeting, May 1, 1809: With an Appendix and a List of Subscribers and Benefactors.* (Philadelphia: Printed by order of the Society; Fry and Kammerer printers, 1809).

See "Timeline History of the Pennsylvania Bible Society," *Pennsylvania Bible Society* (http://pabible.org/timeline_history.html, November 17, 2015).

Under the leadership of Bishop Francis Asbury, American Methodism initiated one of the most important institutions in maintaining the Christian principles that birthed America—the Sunday School.[90] Because of his association with Methodism, it is not surprising that Dr. Rush became a leader in the Sunday School movement. Rush again worked with Dr. White, to establish Sunday schools in Philadelphia,

Francis Asbury

a movement which became the forerunner of the all-important American Sunday School Union, which helped to perpetuate the American republic upon biblical principles.[91] Many of America's Founding Fathers knew that the republican form of government given to America could only be sustained upon the principles of the Bible. For this reason, many became active in training the next generation of American patriots through the institution of the Sunday School.

In an appropriate summary of the life of Dr. Rush, one of his biographers reflected upon the formative influence of his Christian convictions upon his character:

> In all the periods of his life he was remarkable for his attention to religious duties and his reverence for the Holy Scriptures. He urges in all his writings, the excellency of the Christian faith and its happy influence upon the social habits of the country. To his students he especially recommends it as one of the . . . [accompanying] excellencies and subsidiary accomplishments of the profession. He omitted no possible occasion of attending upon church himself,

---

[90] Morris, *Civil Institutions of the United States*, 453.

[91] See this article for details: Stephen Flick, "Sunday School Perpetuates American Republic," *Christian Heritage Fellowship* (http://christianheritagefellowship.com/sunday-school-preserves-american-republic/, April 22, 2015).

and considered the observance of the Sabbath, even as a civil institution, a most rational policy. On the Sabbath he observes not only refection [refreshment] is given to those who are wasted by fatigues, but the idle are diverted from unprofitable or vicious amusements; they not only acquire pious sentiments, but contract those amiable and decorous habits which dignify and adorn private society. When men of conspicuous reputation neglected the ordinances of the Sabbath, he considered them very justly as mischievous to the community; for men who impair the honest and decent manners of a state are not less criminal than they who trample upon its laws and institutions.[92]

Not one of the three most important Founding Fathers believed that the Bible should be removed from the public or fail to have an influence upon the government of America. The idea that the Ten Commandments should be removed from public property would have been an abhorrent idea to all of America's Founding Fathers! And, the notion that public school children should be prohibited from being taught the Bible would have evoked strong condemnation from them as well. How do we know this? Secularists and the irreligious edit textbooks to remove the Christian sentiments of America's Founding Fathers. They know that both the public or state papers and the original private writings of the Founding Fathers are filled with biblical references, allusions, and clear teachings they wished their posterity to enjoy and follow.

> Dr. Rush wrote one of the strongest arguments for the use of the Bible as a schoolbook. You may read this brief work below in its entirety, under the heading, "Reading 1: Defense of the Use of the Bible as a Schoolbook," found on page 91.

---

[92] Sanderson, *Signers of the Declaration of Independence*, 4:283.

After the American Revolution

Additional subjects could be discussed that further demonstrate that America's Founding Fathers did not believe that the Christian faith should be denied influence upon the government and moral direction of the nation. For example, an historical study of the subject of chaplains in government—and many other subjects—would further demonstrate that America's Founding Fathers knew that if the republican principles of the Bible were marginalized, the tyranny that secularism produces would again raise its ugly head. America's Founding Fathers never believed the Christian cross should be denied a place at an American war memorial or veterans' gravesite. Nor did they believe American children should be denied the right to have the Bible read in school, that prayer should be disallowed at a public graduation or football game, nor did they believe a nativity scene at Christmas should be denied a place on the town square.

From the earliest days of the Continental Congress—when the decision was made to begin their sessions with prayer—the Christian faith was welcome in the decisions of Congress, but for the most part, Congress recognized the rights of states to regulate matters of religion. In fact, of the thirteen original states, eleven of them had state churches that received the endorsement and support of the colonies or states.[93] While the Continental Congress did not endorse any single denomination, it did, nevertheless, accord a place to Christianity that it did not grant to

---

[93] Galloway, 140.

other religions. However, the states were far less reserved in their support of Christianity. In discussing the Christian faith of America's Founding Fathers, only a portion of the narrative is told when only their expressions of faith at the congressional or federal level are related; far more attention could be given to the way in which the Founding Fathers expressed their faith at governmental levels within their respective states.

However, there is a personal side of the discussion that also needs to be told, which further amplifies our appreciation for their roles in government—whether at the national or state levels. Once again, the subjects to be considered must be limited; it is not possible to fully explain all of the ways in which they expressed their Christian faith in the communities in which they lived. Yet, thumbnail sketches of specific ways they attempted to pass on their Christian faith to succeeding generations will allow contemporary Americans to consider and appreciate what secularists seek to obscure and deny. In the following pages, two examples of the institutions America's Founding Fathers initiated and two examples of individuals who were instrumental in their inceptions and perpetuation will briefly be considered. These institutions were important to the Founding Fathers because they were regarded as a means of furthering the principles of the Bible that had given birth to America. They believed that only the Christian principles that birthed America were capable of maintaining vibrant national life, and for this reason, they sought to entrust it to the next generation through institutions that could achieve this goal.

Voltaire (Francois-Marie Arouet)

The Founding Fathers and Sunday School

Following the American Revolution, spiritual and moral life in the new nation plummeted. Pastors or lay leaders of local churches often led the Minute Men and were on the frontline of the American Revolution. Given the fact that American Christian leaders were compelled by their biblical convictions to oppose King George III in the Revolution, the Church in America experienced a vacuum in leadership following the War of Independence. Because so many Christian leaders had been killed in the Revolution, local churches were often left to leaders who had little or no spiritual qualifications. French soldiers who came to fight for the American cause often brought with them the seeds of atheism, agnosticism, and various influences of infidelity that had been sown in France through Voltaire, Rousseau, and the Encyclopedists or French Intellectuals. The era following the Revolution was one of the darkest eras in American history.

Seven years of war had a debilitating spiritual influence upon the American colonies. Methodists, who along with the Baptists were the most evangelistic, were losing nearly four thousand a year due to the spiritual lethargy that settled upon young America.[94] As early as 1765, much of France had embraced infidelity due to the abuses of the Roman church in that country. Protestants were also treated with contempt. In the latter part of the eighteenth century, the American colonies experienced a dramatic disinterest in religion and morality. French infidelity swept through the colonies through the French soldiers who had been allied with America.

Founding Father, President John Adams, understood what many in America today adamantly seek to deny—that the principles of Christianity were responsible for the birth of America. Adams was one of the most influential Founding Fathers, providing a leading voice in the formation of the Declaration of Independence and contributing important thoughts

John Adams

---

[94] J. Edwin Orr, *The Eager Feet: Evangelical Awakenings, 1790-1830* (Chicago: Moody Press, 1975), 1-12.

on the nature of government with his pamphlet, "Thoughts on Government"—which was particularly influential in the formation of state constitutions. On June 28, 1813, John Adams penned a letter to Thomas Jefferson. In this letter, Mr. Adams clearly identified the influential role that the Christian faith played in the formation of America as an independent nation, writing:

> The general principles on which the [American Founding] fathers achieved independence were the only principles in which that beautiful assembly of young men could unite . . . And what were these general principles? I answer, the general principles of Christianity, in which all those sects were united, and the general principles of English and American liberty, in which all those young men united, and which had united all parties in America, in majorities sufficient to assert and maintain her independence. Now I will avow, that I then believed and now believe that those general principles of Christianity are as eternal and immutable as the existence and attributes of God; and that those principles of liberty are as unalterable as human nature and our terrestrial, mundane system.[95]

John Adams and the other Founding Fathers were well aware that the American republic had been birthed by the principles of Christianity, and if the republic was to be enjoyed by succeeding generations of Americans, the Christian principles that established the nation must be given by one generation to the next. How the Christian principles that established America were to be passed on to succeeding generations

---

[95] John Adams, *The Works of John Adams, Second President of the United States: with a Life of the Author, Notes and Illustrations, by his Grandson Charles Francis Adams* (Boston: Little, Brown and Co., 1856). 10 volumes. Vol. 10. [Online] available from http://oll.libertyfund.org/titles/2127; accessed 8/11/2014; Internet. John Adams to Thomas Jefferson, June 28, 1813.

of Americans soon became a matter of considerable effort by many prominent Americans.

Recognizing the spiritual demise that was all around them, Christians became earnest about the state of the nation, and as a result of their renewed spiritual interest, America experienced the Second Great Awakening. In New England in the 1790s, a grandson of Jonathan Edwards— who was so instrumental in the First Great Awakening—began to address the secularism that threatened the life of the

Timothy Dwight

American republic. Following in his grandfather's footsteps, Timothy Dwight embarked upon a vigorous campaign to exterminate secularism or infidelity on the campus of Yale College soon after becoming president in 1795. In his class disputation on the question, "Is the Bible the Word of God," Dwight was influential in converting many students.[96] Another effort in which a number of Founding Fathers participated to turn their young nation back to the Christian principles that founded the nation was the American Sunday School Union.

While various efforts to catechize and provide biblical instruction to Christians throughout the history of the Church have been recorded in the pages of Church history, credit for the rise and use of the "Sunday school" belongs to Methodism.[97] Though generally credit is given to Anglican layman, Robert Raikes for beginning the Sunday school, proper credit goes to a Methodist by the name of Hannah Ball for conceiving and beginning this important spiritual institution. In the British Isles and early America, the Methodists—like most Christians— were deeply concerned about proper Christian education. Hannah Ball began her Sunday school in High Wycombe, England in 1769, and

---

[96] Lyman Beecher and Charles Beecher, *Autobiography, Correspondence, Etc., of Lyman Beecher, D.D.* (New York: Harper, 1864).

[97] *Dictionary of National Biography*, (1885–1900), "Ball, Hannah."

upon her death, the administration of her school fell upon her sister, Anne.

Not until July 1780 in Gloucester, England did Robert Raikes begin his well-known Sunday schools, in the home of Mrs. Meredith. In 1784, Raikes penned a letter that was published in the Methodist periodical, *Arminian Magazine,* and very likely was influential in the beginning of Sunday schools among the Methodists in America. By 1786, Methodist American bishop, Francis Asbury, began to use Sunday schools within his Methodist churches.[98] But the Methodists in fledgling America did not remain isolated in their use of the Sunday school. By the early nineteenth century, Methodism joined other evangelical Christian churches in an attempt to evangelize and educate America through the use of the Sunday school. As will emerge in the discussion below, some of the most prominent names in America became advocates of the American Sunday School, realizing that the character of the American Republic rested upon the moral and spiritual shoulders of the generations of Americans that succeeded them. For this reason, they became strong advocates of various means of disseminating biblical truth. They believed that in this way, the evangelical, life-changing influence of the Bible could regenerate individual lives, which in turn could regenerate the family, the church, commercial interests, and all society.

The first chaplain of the American Continental Congress was Rev. Jacob Duche, the rector of the Anglican, Christ Church,[99] appointed by Congress in

Jacob Duche

---

[98] H. Bernard in the *American Journal of Education* in the Library of Congress places this date as early as 1783, but this is unlikely. Methodist historians place the point of origin at Granger's and Thomas Crenshaw's—which were the same place. See Francis Asbury, *The Journal and Letters of Francis Asbury* (Nashville: Abingdon Press, 1958), 1:349.

[99] Christ Church, because of its important role in the emergence of America, became known as "the Nation's Church."

September, 1774.[100] Because of its influential role upon Congress and the formation of the nation, Christ Church became known as "The Nation's Church."[101] Three years later, in September 1777, the British occupied Philadelphia, and Rev. Duche was arrested, and upon his release from British custody, wrote an impassioned letter to General George Washington, pleading with him to lay down his arms and negotiate a peace with the British. For this, Duche was convicted of high treason by the State of Pennsylvania and fled to England, not returning to America until 1792. One of his successors to both his pastorate at Christ Church and the Continental Congress was Rev. Dr. William White, who was to become one of the most influential leaders in establishing those institutions that would perpetuate Christianity in America.

On October 1, 1777, the Continental Congress appointed two chaplains to assume the place Rev. Duche vacated as chaplain upon fleeing to England. They were Rev. Dr. William White (Duche's successor at Christ Episcopal Church) and George Duffield, pastor of the Third Presbyterian Church of Philadelphia. It should be noted that from the very beginning of America's "federal" government, Congress began to practice the correct interpretation of

William White

"separation of church and state." That is, no single denomination of orthodox Christians would be permitted to dominate the life of the federal government, though orthodox Christianity would be allowed to influence the moral and legal life of the nation. However, states were

---

[100] Rev. Duche was summoned to Carpenter Hall, Philadelphia, Pennsylvania on September 7, 1774. He read from Psalm 35 and offered an extemporaneous prayer that deeply affected the members of Congress.

[101] Catherine Millard, *The Rewriting of America's History* (Camp Hill, PA: Horizon House Publishers, 1991), 259.

free to decide concerning whether they would have state churches—without federal intervention—in matters related to religion.[102]

The year after Congress convened for the first time under the new Constitution, a group of prominent Christians convened a meeting that helped to ensure that the Christian principles that birthed America would be given to succeeding generations of Americans. On December 19, 1790, Rev. William White (pastor and chaplain of Congress), Dr. Benjamin Rush,[103] Matthew Carey, Thomas P. Cope, and

Benjamin Rush

other prominent Christians gathered in Philadelphia, Pennsylvania "for the purpose of taking into consideration the establishment of Sunday Schools in this city."[104] The day after Christmas, on December 26, this gathering of concerned leaders adjourned following the adoption of a constitution for their newly formed society. Less than two weeks later, on January 11, 1791, they reconvened again to continue their efforts. Officers were elected and the organization of the society was finalized. The name given to their society, though lengthy, was descriptive of their efforts: "Society for the Institution and Support of First-day or Sunday Schools in the City of Philadelphia,"[105] and was composed of different evangelical Christian denominations. Rev. Dr. White was selected as

---

[102] Eleven of the thirteen states had "state churches" at the time the federal Constitution was composed and ratified. The First Amendment was a guarantee to those states that they would not have their authority usurped by the federal government.

[103] Dr. Benjamin Rush was a signer of the Declaration of Independence and prominent laborer in the cause of America's freedom. Above all, Dr. Rush was a deeply committed evangelical Christian.

[104] Wm. H. Levering, *The American Sunday School Union, Its Origin, History and Work* (Chicago: Brown, Pettibone & Co., Printers, 1888), 1.

[105] In 1797, the name "First-day of Sunday School Society of Philadelphia" was the name provided for an act of incorporation. Levering, *American Sunday School Union Origin*, 1.

the first president of the society, and through the dedicated efforts of many committed believers, the society began to flourish. Published reports of 1810, 1816, and 1826 disclosed commendable progress in the effort of evangelizing the youth of Philadelphia. The Sunday School Society of Philadelphia "was the first Sunday School society organized in the country for missionary work."[106]

Through the influence of the Philadelphia Sunday school society, other similar societies were initiated in other states. One of the most prominent individuals to catch a vision for the work of the Sunday school movement was Eleazar Lord, an American author, educator, founder of the Manhattan Insurance Company, and the first president of the Erie Railroad. Having studied at Princeton College and

Eleazar Lord

Andover Seminary, Eleazar acquired an interest in Christian missions. Though he never became a foreign missionary, Eleazar came to regard the Sunday school movement as a mission endeavor, spending a significant portion of the year 1815 in Philadelphia, learning from the Sunday School Society there. Returning to New York, Eleazar helped to organize "The New York Sunday School Union" on February 26, 1816.[107] That same year, he was a member of the convention that organized the American Bible Society in New York City. The New York Sunday School Union quickly distinguished itself, assuming a prominent role in the developments that followed from the Sunday school movement:

> To this New York society more than to any other, it is said, we are indebted for the promulgation of the wide-spread union principle, since the first suggestion

[106] Levering, *American Sunday School Union Origin*, 1-2.
[107] Levering, *American Sunday School Union Origin*, 2.

of a national Sunday School Union came from this society.[108]

Though the idea of a national Sunday school union appears to have originated with representatives from New York, the suggestion was acted upon in Philadelphia. In 1817, the Philadelphia Sunday school society organized an adult version of the Sunday school, named the "Philadelphia Sunday and Adult School Union," at which time an annual meeting was also established, to which other state societies sent representatives. In addition to the New York Sunday school society, other societies had also been formed. Representatives from other Sunday school societies were present at the seventh annual meeting at Philadelphia when plans were laid to unite the various societies and unions into a national organization. A constitution was developed, and the following resolution was placed before the assembled representatives:

> Whereas, The great and progressing increase of Sabbath [Sunday] Schools throughout our country, exerting a powerful and most beneficial influence over all classes of society, calls loudly for union and organized action; and the prosperity of this institution clearly shows the efficiency of such union; and Whereas, the Constitution of the American Sunday School Union has been approved by the Sunday and Adult School Union, of Philadelphia, and other unions; therefore, Resolved, That the Constitution of the American Sunday School Union be adopted.[109]

With the adoption of the resolution and constitution, the various Sunday school societies of each state were united into the American Sunday School Union (ASSU).

---

[108] Levering, *American Sunday School Union Origin*, 2.
[109] Levering, *American Sunday School Union Origin*, 4.

Being so far removed from this momentous effort, those of us living in the twenty-first century can scarcely begin to understand the impact that the American Sunday School Union exercised upon the life of young America. Prominent national figures caught the Christian evangelical vision that was cast by the Union and were quickly persuaded to lend their support to an effort that would further the American republic with Christian morality. Among the most distinguished to serve were long-time vice president, Pennsylvania Governor James Pollock who, as director of the United States Mint in Philadelphia, first inscribed American currency with "In God We Trust"; Supreme Court Justice, Bushrod Washington, nephew of George Washington; Supreme Court Chief Justice, John Marshall; author of our national anthem, Francis Scott Key; American statesman, Daniel Webster; and later, D. L. Moody, the well-known evangelist; John Adams, relative of both early American presidents and organizer of more than 320 Sunday schools; Laura Ingalls Wilder, author of the *Little House on the Prairie* novel series; and others concerned about Christianizing the youth of America and the perpetuation of the American republic—to say nothing of those distinguished Americans already mentioned.[110]

One of the greatest influences the American Sunday School Union exercised over America was the distribution of Christian literature. Juvenile religious literature was a priority for the ASSU. Typical of this massive effort was the book, *Life of Washington* by Anna C. Reed (referenced above), which unfolded the Christian life of George Washington. For more than 150 years, the ASSU printed and distributed books, hymnals, tracts, and tickets to reward Scripture memorization. Their "Ten-Dollar Libraries" was an affordable set of 100 books that provided teaching materials for Sunday schools and often were the only lending library of many communities.

The first paid missionary was hired in 1821 and an aggressive development program undertaken throughout the remainder of the

---

[110] Anna Reed and American Sunday-School Union., *The Life of Washington* (Green Forest, AR: Attic Books, 2009), 4.

nineteenth century. In 1888, historian of the ASSU, William Levering, wrote,

> During the past 64 years, the union has organized an average of 1,280 new Sunday Schools a year...[111]

Before 1890, the International Secretary reported 8,034,478 scholars in attendance in all the Sunday schools in the United States, but the chairman of the Executive Committee stated that a more accurate number would be closer to 8,436,201.[112] Using the 1880 census report of 50,189,209, statistics indicate that nearly six percent of the population of the United States was attending Sunday schools sponsored by the ASSU.

In 1830, the Sunday School Union embarked upon a vision to start a Sunday school in every town in the Mississippi Valley. An amazing story is told about one of the missionaries who was responsible for helping to achieve that vision. "Stuttering Stephen" Paxson had overcome the double handicaps of a stammer and a limp to become a successful hatter in Winchester, Illinois. But Stephen was also the favorite fiddler for the Saturday night square dance.

One Sunday morning, Mary, Stephen's daughter, who had been told by her Sunday school teacher that she would get a star if she brought a new scholar to Sunday school, decided that the new student would be her father. The tired fiddler granted his daughter's request and accompanied her to Sunday school. He found himself seated in a class of boys who were helping him to pronounce the hard words in their Bible lesson. It was not long before Paxson's fiddle was a welcomed part of the Sunday school exercises. God placed his finger upon Paxson's heart, called him to salvation in Christ, and laid upon his heart the vision to evangelize the Mississippi Valley. He moved his family into the Mississippi Valley and set out on horseback to establish Sunday

---

[111] Levering, *American Sunday School Union Origin*, 4-5.
[112] Levering, *American Sunday School Union Origin*, 9.

schools. Over the next twenty-five years, Stuttering Stephen Paxson traveled 100,000 miles, touching 83,000 children with the gospel and establishing 1,314 Sunday schools.[113] Today, towns, cemeteries, churches and other icons of the American landscape bear the name "Union." Most of us fail to realize that these places bear silent witness to the fact that Baptists, Methodists, Presbyterians, and other evangelical denominations once united their hearts and voices in these places for the sake of disseminating the truth of God's Word.

Upon arriving in America, the Pilgrim Fathers realized that their efforts to evangelize the native Indians were most effective when addressed toward the children.[114] Soon after America became an independent nation, some of the most prominent American Founding Fathers gave themselves to the evangelization of the nation through the American Sunday School Union, knowing that the republic they had helped to birth would be short lived if succeeding generations could not appreciate the Christian principles that birthed and shaped the nation.[115] They realized that the best way to perpetuate the American republic was to evangelize younger generations. What the Pilgrim Fathers and America's Founding Fathers realized is every bit as valid in the twenty-first century. If America is to return to Christ, the most vigorous efforts must be extended toward the youth. John Adams realized that Christianity had birthed America and the leaders of the American Sunday School Union realized that the principles of Christianity had birthed the nation and must continue to perpetuate its life.

[113] Elmer Towns, *The Successful Sunday School and Teachers Guidebook* (Carol Stream IL: Creation House, 1976), 338-339.

[114] William Bradford, *Of Plymouth Plantation: Bradford's History of the Plymouth Settlement, 1608-1650* (Bulverde TX: Mantle Ministries, 1998), 138.

[115] See Dr. Benjamin Rush's on this subject beginning on page 48.

Bible Societies and the President of Congress

Other important institutions that continued to breathe the Christian principles that had birthed America into succeeding generations of Americas were Bible societies. The modern Bible society movement began in 1804 with the founding of the British and Foreign Bible Society in London but soon leaped the Atlantic to quickly spread throughout America because of America's Founding Fathers.[116] On November 10, 1808, Robert Ralston, a prominent merchant and philanthropist in Philadelphia wrote a letter to a friend in England, Josiah Roberts, expressing his desire to start a Bible Society in America. Mr. Ralston did not have long to wait. On December 12, 1808, the first formal meeting of the Bible Society of Philadelphia was convened, selecting Bishop William White—chaplain of Congress—as the first president and Dr. Benjamin Rush as the first vice president. In 1840, this first Bible society in America renamed itself to the Pennsylvania Bible Society.[117] By 1809, at least seven new Bible societies had been formed, including New York, Connecticut, Massachusetts, Maine and New Jersey, and by 1816, at least 130 Bible societies were organized in twenty-four states or territories—fifteen of which were "women's" societies.[118]

Elias Boudinot

One of the leading voices in the Bible society movement was Elias Boudinot, American patriot of the American Revolution and President of the Continental Congress. Elias Boudinot was born in Philadelphia,

---

[116] Prior to this, the Society for the Propagation of Christian Knowledge (SPCK, founded in 1698) and the Society for the Propagation of the Gospel (SPG, founded in 1701) attempted to provide Bibles to English readers in Britain and her colonies. D. Ewert, "Bible Societies," *Dictionary of Christianity in America*. eds. Daniel Reid, et al. Downers Grove, IL: Intervarsity Press, 1990.

[117] "Timeline History of the Pennsylvania Bible Society," *Pennsylvania Bible Society* (http://pabible.org/timeline_history.html, November 23, 2015).

[118] Ewert, "Bible Societies."

Pennsylvania on May 2, 1740 to Elias Boudinot III, a merchant and silversmith, who was a neighbor and friend of Benjamin Franklin. His mother, Mary Catherine Williams, was born in the British West Indies of Welsh ancestry. Elias's paternal great-grandparents, Jean Boudinot and Marie Suire of Marans, Aunis, France, were Huguenots (French Calvinistic Protestants) who fled to New York about 1687 to avoid the persecution many Protestants experienced at the hands of King Louis XIV.[119]

The Boudinot family became firmly interwoven with other leading families of the American Revolution. Nine children were born to Elias's parents, Mary Catherine and Elias Boudinot Sr., but of these, only the younger Elias and his three siblings, Annis, Mary, and Elisha, survived to adulthood. Annis distinguished herself as one of the first published women poets in the Thirteen Colonies, while brother Elisha Boudinot became the Chief Justice of the Supreme Court of New Jersey. In addition to these distinctions, sister Annis married Richard Stockton, one of the fifty-six signers of the Declaration of Independence.

Into the War of Independence, Boudinot threw his life's energy. In 1775, he was elected to the New Jersey provincial assembly, and like all patriots, his thoughts were continually upon the support of the American cause. As the War of Independence was engaged, he loaned field commanders money to purchase desperately needed supplies for American forces and actively supported the efforts of American spies. His participation in the committee of correspondence no doubt was the natural bridge into American spying efforts.

On May 5, 1777, General George Washington asked Boudinot to accept the office of Commissary General for Prisoners, which managed enemy prisoners and supplied American prisoners held captive by the British. Congress concurred with his appointment, and Boudinot was

---

[119] "Elias Boudinot," *Wikipedia* (https://en.wikipedia.org/wiki/Elias_Boudinot, October 12, 2015).

granted a commission as colonel in the American Continental Army, giving him military authority to conduct his duties.

He held his office as Commissary General for only a relatively short period of time. In November 1777, the legislature of New Jersey appointed him as a state delegate to the Second Continental Congress, but his duties as Commissary prevented him from attending. In May 1778, he resigned his office as Commissary and by July 7, 1778, he was able to attend his first session of Congress, from which place he continued to seek the welfare of prisoners of war.

With his first term in Congress ending at the close of 1778, he did not return to Congress until 1781, at which time he served in this office until 1783 when the term expired. One of the great distinctions of his life was experienced in Congress when he served from 1782 to 1783 as President of Congress. But, additional distinction was received when, as President of Congress, he was called upon to sign the treaty of peace with England, known as the Paris Peace Treaty (in 1783).

With American independence won, Elias returned to his law practice, but, like George Washington, he was called once again to serve his country. Once the United States Constitution was ratified in 1789, he was elected from New Jersey to the United States House of Representatives to serve in the First, Second, and Third Congresses (from March 4, 1789 to March 3, 1795), but refused to be re-nominated for the Fourth Congress. The same year he stepped down from Congress, President Washington nominated him as the second Director of the Mint, in which capacity he served from 1795 to 1805.

One of Boudinot's legacies to America occurred during his first term in the House of Representatives under the Constitution. On Friday September 25, 1789, Mr.

Federal Hall and Trinity Church 1789

Boudinot made a motion on the floor of the House of Representatives that would eventually help establish America's annual Thanksgiving. The details of his motion relate the fact that the Founding Fathers, indeed, wove their Christian convictions into the life of American government—a fact clearly recorded in the minutes of Congress:

> Mr. Boudinot said, he could not think of letting the session [of Congress] pass over without offering an opportunity to all the citizens of the United States of joining, with one voice, in returning to Almighty God their sincere thanks for the many blessings he had poured down upon them. With this view, therefore, he would move the following resolution:
>
> *Resolved*, That a joint committee of both Houses be directed to wait upon the President of the United States, to request that he would recommend to the people of the United States a day of public thanksgiving and prayer, to be observed by acknowledging, with grateful hearts, the many signal favors of Almighty God, especially by affording them an opportunity peaceably to establish a Constitution of government for their safety and happiness.
>
> Mr. Burke did not like this mimicking of European customs, where they made a mere mockery of thanksgivings. Two parties at war frequently sung **Te Deum** for the same event, though to one it was a victory, and to the other a defeat.
>
> Mr. Boudinot was sorry to hear arguments drawn from the abuse of a good thing against the use of it. He hoped no gentleman would make a serious opposition to a measure both prudent and just.

Mr. Tucker thought the House had no business to interfere in a matter which did not concern them. Why should the President direct the people to do what, perhaps, they have no mind to do? They may not be inclined to return thanks for a Constitution until they have experienced that it promotes their safety and happiness. We do not yet know but they may have reason to be dissatisfied with the effects it has already produced; but whether this be so or not, it is a business with which Congress have nothing to do; it is a religious matter, and, as such, is proscribed to us. If a day of thanksgiving must take place, let it be done by the authority of the several States; they know best what reason their constituents have to be pleased with the establishment of this Constitution.

Mr. Sherman justified the practice of thanksgiving, on any signal event, not only as a laudable one in itself, but as warranted by a number of precedents in holy writ: for instance, the solemn thanksgivings and rejoicings which took place in the time of Solomon, after the building of the temple, was a case in point. This example, he thought, worthy of Christian imitation on the present occasion; and he would agree with the gentleman who moved the resolution.

Mr. Boudinot quoted further precedents from the practice of the late Congress [and how this had been done on four occasions]; and hoped the motion would meet a ready acquiescence.

The question was now put on the resolution, and it was carried in the affirmative; and Messrs. Boudinot, Sherman, and Sylvester were appointed a committee

> on the part of the House [to take the request for a day
> of Thanksgiving to President Washington].[120]

At this very first session of Congress under the United States Constitution, Elias Boudinot helped to initiate the first Presidential Thanksgiving Proclamation. Given the fact that it had been a practice of the Continental Congress to issue both fast and thanksgiving day proclamations (as previously discussed), he would not have regarded the request to issue this proclamation as anything new. In fact, several years earlier, on Saturday, October 18, 1783, a congressional committee, composed of James Duane, Samuel Huntington, and Samuel Holten, submitted a draft of a thanksgiving day proclamation to fellow members of the Continental Congress which was approved and signed by its president, non-other than Elias Boudinot![121]

Just as Benjamin Franklin sought to refute the irreligion of Thomas Paine, so Boudinot reflected the general sentiment of other Founding Fathers when he also formally refuted Paine's secularism. In fact, the Continental Congress denounced secularism when in the fast day proclamation of Saturday, March 11, 1780 it announced that one of the purposes of the proclamation was

> . . . to banish vice and irreligion from among us, and
> establish virtue and piety by his Divine grace . . .[122]

When have Americans ever been informed of the fact that one of the earliest intents of America's Congresses was "to banish vice and irreligion"? Whereas Paine's first significant political work, *Common Sense*,[123] employed arguments based upon the Bible, his subsequent works *The Rights of Man* and *Age of Reason* were decidedly secular

---

[120] *The Debates and Proceedings in the Congress of the United States With an Appendix Containing Important State Papers and Public Documents and All the Laws of a Public Nature: With a Copious Index.* Washington [D.C.]: 1:949-950.

[121] *Journals of the Continental Congress*, 25:699-701

[122] *Journals of the Continental Congress*, 16:253

[123] *Common Sense* was first published in January 1776.

and irreligious. Paine published his *Age of Reason* in three parts, the first two parts were published in 1794 and 1795 and the third part, he published in 1807. Founding Fathers who had welcomed and supported Paine when he immigrated to America from England soon turned against him for having attacked Christianity in the *Age of Reason*. In fact, after receiving a manuscript of *Age of Reason* from Paine before its publication, Benjamin Franklin pleaded with Paine not to publish it.[124] With other Founding Fathers, Boudinot was incensed by Paine's *Age of Reason* and openly challenged Paine by publishing his own response in 1801 titled, *The Age of Revelation, or The Age Of Reason Shown to Be an Age of Infidelity*. In his book, Boudinot not only demonstrated his contempt for Paine's irreligion but also disclosed the contempt that America's Founding Fathers had for secular infidelity and deism.[125]

---

[124] After reading Paine's manuscript of *Age of Reason*, Mr. Franklin responded, urging him not to publish it. Jared Sparks, *The Works of Benjamin Franklin* (Boston: Tappan, Whittemore, and Mason, 1840), 10:281-282; quoted in "Benjamin Franklin's letter to Thomas Paine," WallBuilders (http://www.wallbuilders.com/libissuesarticles.asp?id=58, April 15, 2015).

[125] In his introduction, Boudinot wrote:

When I first took up this treatise, I considered it as one of those vicious and absurd publications, filled with ignorant declamation and ridiculous representations of simple facts, the reading of which, with attention, would be an undue waste of time; but afterwards, finding it often the subject of conversation, in all ranks of society, and knowing the author to be generally plausible in his language, and very artful in turning the clearest truths into ridicule, I determined to read it, with an honest design of impartially examining into its real merits.

I confess, that I was much mortified to find, the whole force of this vain man's genius and art, pointed at the youth of America, and her unlearned citizens, (for I have no doubt, but that it was originally intended for them) in hopes of raising a skeptical temper and disposition in their minds, well knowing that this was the best inlet to infidelity, and the most effectual way of serving its cause, thereby sapping the foundation of our holy religion in their minds.

. . .

. . . be assured . . . [reader] that this author's whole work, is made up of old objections, [that have already been] answered, and that conclusively, [answered] a thousand times over, by the advocates for our holy religion. Some of them he has

The notable expression of Boudinot's Christian faith in his most mature years occurred in relation to the formation of the American Bible Society. In poor health, Elias Boudinot was burdened for a "general Bible society" that could distribute the Bible throughout America and around the world.

As previously observed, by 1816 many state and local Bible societies existed, but Boudinot's vision for a Bible society was broader and universal in scope. In a letter to William Jay, the son of John Jay, America's first Chief Justice of the Supreme Court, Boudinot helped to lay the plans for what was to become the American Bible Society. The true Christian spirit of Boudinot and most of

William Jay

the Founding Fathers was reflected in his motivation to organize the society:

> I wish to promote a principle of perfect equality of right, universal Brotherly love, founded on Gospel purity, and where we cannot agree to unite, we may agree to differ in peace and good will. I consider the present call to enter into our Lord's vineyard, as laborers, tho' at the eleventh hour, to be one of the most encouraging opportunities and imperious calls that ever has been conferred on the Christian

---

endeavored to clothe with new language, and put into a more ridiculous form; but many of them he has collected almost word for word, from the writings of the deists of the last and present century. Elias Boudinot, *The Age of Revelation, or, the Age of Reason Shewn to be an Age of Infidelity* (Philadelphia: Asbury Dickins, 1801), xii, xiv, xv.

professor to promote the glory of God and the best interest of his fellow men.[126]

---

[126] In a letter to William Jay dated April 4, 1816, Boudinot wrote:

My dear Sir:

By the blessing of Almighty God, after near Six Months close confinement, I am permitted to set up in my Bed, for 3 Hours in the Day. These precious moments, I have devoted to a full consideration of one of the greatest & most interesting subjects (a general Bible Society) that has ever honored the Children of Men. Weak and feeble, scarcely able to think or write, my Efforts promised but little in the great Cause, when your welcome & unexpected Letter of the 2nd Ultimo was brought in. My-drooping Spirits were raised—my Heart was indeed cheered and my mind greatly revived. I could not help giving glory to God for the great Encouragement afforded me to press on in this glorious Cause, when I thus beheld his special Mercy in raising up so powerful a support in this joyous work & Labor of Love. Tho' it is not more than 2 Hours since I received it, I am attempting to scribble a few lines of acknowledgment and gratitude for your excellent memoir. I fear you will not be able to read it, being among my first essays in letter writing and rather against medical advice. I have already sent for a Printer to engage him to publish the memoir without delay, but I wish to have your candid opinion on my Idea of changing a few sentences of the constitution. I have prepared a very rough draught of one which greatly coincides with yours in the leading points, ...

...

I wish to promote a principle of perfect equality of right, universal Brotherly love, founded on Gospel purity, and where we cannot agree to unite, we may agree to differ in peace and good will. I consider the present call to enter into our Lord's vineyard, as laborers, tho' at the eleventh hour, to be one of the most encouraging opportunities and imperious calls that ever has been conferred on the Christian professor to promote the glory of God and the best interest of his fellow men.

...

Pardon, dear Sir, the garrulity of an old man who even forgets his extreme weakness and the prohibitions of his physician. Forgive his blunders and incorrectness, for he is almost exhausted. I can Only again express my obligations to you and subscribe myself with great sincerity.

Yours most Affectionately,

Elias Boudinot

"Letter from Elias Boudinot to William Jay on the Founding of a General Bible Society, Dated April 4, 1816," *American Bible History* (http://www.americanbiblehistory.com/boudinot-jay-letter.html, October 16, 2015).

Stephen A. Flick, Ph.D.

More than a month after Boudinot composed this letter to William Jay, a meeting was convened in New York City to organize "a general Bible Society" in America, and on May 11, 1816, the newly formed American Bible Society elected Elias Boudinot as its first president. Boudinot served in this capacity until his death five years later.

John Jay

Beginning with Elias Boudinot, some very distinguished Americans have occupied the presidency of the American Bible Society. From the beginning of the American Bible Society, the first Chief Justice of the Supreme Court, John Jay, was a member. At the beginning of the Society, Chief Justice Jay was elected vice-president, and at the death of Elias Boudinot in 1821, Jay was elected president. Other distinguished presidents include Frederick Theodore Frelinghuysen—distinguished lawyer, United States Senator, and Secretary of State, Daniel Coit Gilman—president of Johns Hopkins University, Edwin Francis Hyde, a former president of the Philharmonic Society of New York, and one of the most distinguished vice-presidents was Francis Scott Key—author of the United States' National Anthem.

The spirit behind Elias Boudinot's motivation to begin the American Bible Society speaks volumes concerning his character, but also is reflective of the Christian character of the overwhelming number of Founding Fathers. One of his letters that relates his intent in this endeavor is presented below. Please see "Reading 2: President of Congress Starts Bible Society" on page 107.

Bible Societies and the Speaker of the House

One final example of the Christian sentiment of America's Founding Fathers is found in one of the speakers of the House of Representatives. Robert Charles Winthrop (May 12 1809 to November 16 1894) was an American lawyer, politician, and philanthropist who at one point in his political career rose to the office of Speaker of the United States House of Representatives. Like most who lived

Robert Winthrop

during the Founding Era of the United States, Winthrop was concerned about the moral character of America's development. Though not considered by most as a Founding Father, Winthrop does represent the influence and legacy that the Founding Fathers exercised upon succeeding generations. Following the example of many Founding Fathers, Winthrop involved himself in the advancement of Christianity in America—particularly through his political influence, oratory, literary endeavors, and the distribution of the Bible.

Born in Boston to Thomas Lindall Winthrop and his wife Elizabeth Bowdoin Temple, he attended the prestigious Latin School of Boston before studying at Harvard University, where he graduated in 1828. After graduating from Harvard, Winthrop studied law with the well-known American statesman, Daniel Webster. As a powerful orator, Daniel Webster left a lasting impression upon

Daniel Webster

the speaking ability of Winthrop. Serving in national politics for forty years, Webster served in the House of Representatives for eight years, in the Senate for nineteen years, and finally as the United States Secretary of State under three presidents.[127] Upon completion of his study of law with Webster, Robert Winthrop was admitted to the bar in 1831 and subsequently established a practice in Boston.

On March 12, 1832, Robert married Elizabeth Cabot Blanchard. Together, Robert and Elizabeth Winthrop had three children. When Elizabeth died after ten years of marriage, Robert married Adele Granger Thayer.

Only a few years after he established his law practice, Winthrop entered into a political career. From 1834 to 1840, he was a member of the lower house of the Massachusetts' legislature, during which time he was chosen speaker in 1838, 1839, and 1840. In 1840, he was elected to the United States Congress, where he served ten years with distinction, earning himself a reputation as an able debater, orator, and parliamentarian. From 1847 to 1849, he held the office of Speaker of the House of Representatives, and in 1850, he was appointed by the governor of Massachusetts to fill Daniel Webster's seat in the senate when Mr. Webster was appointed Secretary of State. When defeated in his bid for election to the senate by a coalition of Democrats and Free-soilers, he turned his efforts to an unsuccessful election bid for the office of governor of Massachusetts. Disappointed in political life, he retired from politics to devote himself to literary, historical, and benevolent interests.[128] While still the Speaker of the House, Winthrop received the distinction of being chosen to deliver the dedicatory speech of the laying of the cornerstone of the Washington Monument on July 4, 1848.[129]

---

[127] "Daniel Webster," *Wikipedia* (https://en.wikipedia.org/wiki/Daniel_Webster, October 27, 2015).

[128] "John Winthrop," *Appletons' Cyclopædia of American Biography* (https://en.wikisource.org/wiki/Appletons'_Cyclop%C3%A6dia_of_American_Biography/Winthrop,_John, October 27, 2015).

[129] The title of his speech was "National Monument to Washington." Robert Winthrop, *Addresses and Speeches on Various Occasions* (Boston: Little, Brown, and Company, 1852), 70-89. Also see, "John Winthrop," *Appletons' Cyclopædia of American Biography* (https://en.wikisource.org/wiki/

He served as the President of the Massachusetts' Bible Society for several years where he advocated his conviction that Christian morality—as derived from the Bible—was necessary to produce a free society.[130] This sentiment was summarized in his 1849 speech, "The Bible," in which he stated, "Men, in a word, must necessarily be controlled either by a power within them or by a power without them; either by the Word of God or by the strong arm of man; either by the Bible or by the bayonet."[131]

You may read the entire speech below—"Reading 3: By the Bible or By the Bayonet," found on page **113**.

Appletons'_Cyclop%C3%A6dia_of_American_Biography/Winthrop,_John, October 27, 2015).

[130] "Daniel Webster," *Wikipedia* (https://en.wikipedia.org/wiki/Daniel_Webster, October 27, 2015).

[131] It should be noted that this speech was delivered while Winthrop was still the Speaker of the House of Representatives. Robert Winthrop, *Addresses and Speeches on Various Occasions* (Boston: Little, Brown, and Company, 1852), 172.

Conclusion: Research
to Renaissance

This brief study of the place of Christianity and its use of the Bible within the development of America's political and national experience is far from exhaustive. Rather, it has been the objective of this writer to provide insight into the intended role of Christianity and the Bible in American political life as advocated by the most influential Founding Fathers. For well over half a century, various forms of irreligion in America have routinely denied the place of influence that the Founding Fathers accorded to the Bible and its teachings, but the historical facts critique this irreligious assessment as naïve and uninformed.

Support of Scholarly Research

The research of two scholars proves the formative influence accorded to the Bible by the Founding Fathers in general. Charles Hyneman was a Distinguished Professor of political science at Indiana University. Together with Donald S. Lutz, Associate Professor of Political Science at the University of Huston, these two professors reviewed an estimated 15,000 political documents from the founding era of America as an independent nation—an era of nearly half a century, extending from 1760 to 1805. Hyneman and Lutz published their findings in the early 1980s, and the results of their ten-year study were not kind to the fallacies of secularists. They showed that the single most often quoted source in the political writings of America's Founding Fathers was the Bible, receiving 34% of the total number of quotes. Donald Lutz summarized their work in his book, *The Origins of American Constitutionalism*, calling attention to the priority given to the Bible by the Founding Fathers:

> The relative influence of European thinkers on American political thought is a large and complex question not to be answered in any but a provisional way here. We can, however, identify the broad trends of influence and which European thinkers need to be especially considered. One means to this end is an examination of the citations in public political literature written between 1760 and 1805. If we ask which book was most frequently cited in that literature, the answer is, the Bible.[132]

Quotations from additional sources did not receive near the attention accorded to the Bible by the Fathers. Baron Charles Montesquieu ranked a distant second with 8.3% of the total quotes, followed by British legal scholar, William Blackstone, at 7.9%, and theologian and political writer, John Locke, was quoted 2.9% of the time in the quotes identified by Hyneman and Lutz.[133] Further, it should be noted that most of the individuals the Founding Fathers quoted in the Hyneman-Lutz study were Christian thinkers and authors. For years, secularists have insisted that irreligious Enlightenment thinkers were the primary source of influence upon the Founding Fathers, but in fact, the radical Enlightenment thinkers had very little impact upon the development of American political life. One of the subsequent articles developed

---

[132] Donald S. Lutz, *The Origin of American Constitutionalism* (Baton Rouge: Louisiana State University Press, 1988), 140.

[133] Lutz, 139-147.

Also see Charles S. Hyneman and Donald S. Lutz, *American Political Writing During the Founding Era, 1760-1805*, 2 vols. (Indianapolis: Liberty Press, 1983).

by Professor Lutz explained that the "First Enlightenment" thinkers were Christian and were credited with 16% of the political citations. The radical thinkers of the "Second Enlightenment," such as Voltaire, Diderot, and Helvetius, garnered only 2% of the citations while members of the "Third Enlightenment" era, typified by Rousseau, Mably, Raynal, and others, received a mere 4% of interest in the citations of the Founding Fathers.[134]

This study by two political science scholars clearly demonstrates dependence upon the Bible for some of the most "innovative" principles that eventually made their way into the United States Constitution. And, what was the source of inspiration for these "innovations"? As was noted in some of their private writings, the Founding Fathers pointed to the Bible as their source of inspiration.

> The general principles on which the fathers achieved independence were the general principles of Christianity. I will avow that I then believed, and now believe, that those general principles of Christianity are as eternal and immutable as the existence and attributes of God.
>
> Without religion, this world would be something not fit to be mentioned in polite company: I mean hell.
>
> —*President John Adams*

America is the longest thriving form of constitutional government in world history. It is a valid question to ask why America's Constitution has survived so long while governments formed under the influence of irreligion have resulted in upheaval and instability. While many examples could be produced, France alone produces a vivid example.

---

[134] Donald Lutz, "The Relative Influence of European Writers on Late Eighteenth-Century American Political Thought," *American Political Science Review* 189 (1984): 189-97.

With the French Revolution beginning in 1789, the godless influence of Voltaire and Rousseau have resulted in nearly twenty constitutions in the political life of France compared to America's one Constitution. This should come as little surprise to those who are aware of the personal tumult of these patron saints of French infidelity. The irreligion of succeeding generations of Europeans is directly attributable to this era and the influence of these irreligious infidels.

An American Renaissance

Historians generally regard the period in Western civilization from the mid-fourteenth to the mid-seventeenth centuries as the era of the Renaissance. But few realize the two competing streams of thought that emerged during this era have persisted down to the present with the same mutual antagonism that characterized their origin. Both streams of thought drew upon previous generations for their inspiration, and for this reason, the expression, *ad fontes,* came to mean "back to the sources." The sources of inspiration for each of the two currents of thought were worlds apart.

South of the Alps—arising primarily from Florence, Italy—the idea of *ad fontes* meant returning to the secular understanding of the Greco-Roman world. It meant the rediscovery of classical Greek philosophy that was characterized by Protagoras' succinct statement, "Man is the measure of all things." From this worldview, secularism in the contemporary world has drawn its inspiration which places mankind and the human race at the center of human existence—as the most important consideration in all of life. This worldview is responsible for the egocentrism and tyranny of all human relationships. But this worldview has been the cause of the world's most tortured groans of agony. The Voltaires and Darwins of the world have been the faces behind the horrors of the French Revolution and the concentration camps of Adolph Hitler. Nowhere in world history has secularism produced peace and prosperity—nowhere!

North of the Alps, *ad fontes* meant something entirely different than it did for the worldview that radiated from Florence. North of the Alps, Church leaders returned to purest streams of biblical Christianity as they gained access to ancient biblical manuscripts and acquired the ability to study the writings of church leaders closest to the lives of Jesus Christ and his Apostles. This worldview places God at the center of human existence and acknowledges that the God that knows how nature works best is the same God that knows how nations work best.

The English settlers who populated the Thirteen Colonies of America were spiritual and ideological descendants of the biblical Renaissance north of the Alps that sought to make God the center of human existence. The public and personal writing of America's Founding Fathers makes this fact abundantly clear, but for nearly a century, the truth concerning America's Christian heritage has been doubted and denied by those who are the ideological descendants of the worldview that developed south of the Alps. The recipe that made America great is clearly recorded in the writings of America's Founding Fathers, and if America is to be great once again, she must follow the same recipe. There must be a return to the pure sources of thought that made America great. There must be *ad fontes*—there must ultimately be a return to the Bible.

READING 1: DEFENSE OF THE USE OF THE BIBLE AS A SCHOOLBOOK

D^{r. Benjamin Rush, one of the three most important Founding Fathers,}
believed deeply that the youth of America must understand and advocate the principles of the Bible if America was to remain a free and prosperous nation.

Because early America had very active ministers who believed King George III had violated God's law, they called for revolt

Benjamin Rush

against the King. For nearly a decade, ministers preached about ways that the King was violating the law of God as revealed in the Bible. Rev. Jeremy Belknap was among those ministers who taught that the King was violating God's laws in the way he was seeking to govern the American Colonies. In 1767, Rev. Belknap became the pastor of the Congregational Church in Dover, New Hampshire. Eight years later, in 1775, some units of the Dover militia were activated following the Battle of Lexington to support the American cause in the Siege of Boston. Rev. Belknap accompanied those militia units to Boston as chaplain to the New Hampshire troops engaged in the siege and remained with them through the next winter. It was to his friend, Rev. Belknap, that Dr. Rush addressed his essay concerning the need for America's youth to be trained in the teachings of the Bible. That essay is presented below in its entirety and reflects not only the academic

*convictions of the clergy, but America's Founding Fathers, among whom
Dr. Rush was one of the most important.*

A Defense of the Use of the Bible as a Schoolbook, Addressed to the Rev. Jeremy Belknap, of Boston

DEAR SIR,

It is now several months, since I promised to give you my reasons for preferring the Bible as a schoolbook, to all other compositions. I shall not trouble you with an apology for my delaying so long to comply with my promise, but shall proceed immediately to the subject of my letter.

Before I state my arguments in favor of teaching children to read by means of the Bible, I shall assume the five following propositions.

I.   That Christianity is the only true and perfect religion, and that in proportion as mankind adopt its principles, and obey its precepts, they will be wise, and happy.

II. That a better knowledge of this religion is to be acquired by reading the Bible, than in any other way.

III. That the Bible contains more knowledge necessary to man in his present state, than any other book in the world.

IV. That knowledge is most durable, and religious instruction most useful, when imparted in early life,

V.   That the Bible, when not read in schools, is seldom read in any subsequent period of life.

Arguments in Favor of the Use of the Bible

My arguments in favor of the use of the Bible as a schoolbook are founded,

I.   In the constitution of the human mind.

1.   The memory is the first faculty which opens in the minds of children. Of how much consequence, then, must it be, to impress it with the great truths of Christianity, before it is pre-occupied with less interesting subjects! As all liquors, which are poured into a cup generally taste of that which first filled it, so all the knowledge, which is added to that which is treasured up in the memory from the Bible, generally receives an agreeable and useful tincture from it.

2.   There is a peculiar aptitude in the minds of children for religious knowledge. I have constantly found them in the first six or seven years of their lives, more inquisitive upon religious subjects, than upon any others: and an ingenious instructor of youth has informed me, that he has found young children more capable of receiving just ideas upon the most difficult tenets of religion, than upon the most simple branches of human knowledge. It would be strange if it were otherwise; for God creates all his means to suit all his ends. There must of course be a fitness between the human mind, and the truths which are essential to its happiness.

3.   The influence of prejudice is derived from the impressions, which are made upon the mind in early life; prejudices are of two kinds, true and false. In a world where false prejudices do so much mischief, it would discover great weakness not to oppose them, by such as are true.

I grant that many men have rejected the prejudices derived from the Bible: but I believe no man ever did do, without having been made wiser of better, by the early operation of these prejudices upon his mind. Every just principle that is to be found in the writings of Voltaire, is borrowed from the Bible: and the morality of the Deists, which has been so much admired and praised, is, I believe, in most cases, the effect of habits, produced by early instruction in the principles of Christianity.

4. We are subject, by a general law in our natures, to what is called habit. Now if the study of the scriptures be necessary to our happiness at any time of our lives, the sooner we begin to read them, the more we shall be attached to them; for it is peculiar to all the acts of habit, to become easy, strong and agreeable by repetition.

5. It is a law in our natures, that we remember longest the knowledge we acquire by the greatest number of our senses. Now a knowledge of the contents of the Bible, is acquired in school by the aid of the eyes and the ears; for children after getting their lessons, always say them to their masters in an audible voice; of course there is a presumption, that this knowledge will be retained much longer than if it had been acquired in any other way.

6. The interesting events and characters, recorded and described in the Old and New Testaments, are accommodated above all others to seize upon all the faculties of the minds of children. The understanding, the memory, the imagination, the passions, and the moral powers, are all occasionally addressed by the various incidents which are contained in those divine books, insomuch that not to be delighted with them, is to be devoid of every principle of pleasure that exists in a sound mind.

7. There is a native love of truth in the human mind. Lord Shaftsbury says, that "truth is so congenial to our minds, that we love even the shadow of it:" and Horace, in his rules for composing an epic poem, establishes the same law in our natures, by advising the "fictions in poetry to resemble truth." Now the Bible contains more truths than any other book in the world: so true is the testimony that it bears of God in his works of creation, providence, and redemption, that it is called truth itself, by way of preeminence above things that are only simply true. How forcibly are we struck with the evidences of truth, in the history of the Jews, above what we discover in the history of other nations? Where do we find a hero, or an historian record his own faults or vices except in

the Old Testament? Indeed, my friend, from some accounts which I have read of the American Revolution, I begin to grow skeptical to all history except to that which is contained in the Bible. Now if this book be known to contain nothing but what is materially true, the mind will naturally acquire a love for it from this circumstance: and from this affection for the truth in other books, and a preference of it in all the transactions of life.

8. There is a wonderful property in the memory, which enables it in old age, to recover the knowledge it had acquired in early life, after it had been apparently forgotten for forty or fifty years. Of how much consequence, then, must it be, to fill the mind with that species of knowledge, in childhood and youth, which, when recalled in the decline of life, will support the soul under the infirmities of age, and smooth the avenues of approaching death? The Bible is the only book which is capable of affording this support to old age; and it is for this reason that we find it resorted to with so much diligence and pleasure by such old people as have read it in early life. I can recollect many instances of this kind in persons who discovered no attachment to the Bible, in the meridian of their lives, who have notwithstanding, spent the evening of them, in reading no other book. The late Sir John Pringle, Physician to the Queen of Great Britain, after passing a long life in camps and at court, closed it by studying the scriptures. So anxious was he to increase his knowledge in them that he wrote to Dr. Michaelis, a learned professor of divinity in Germany, for an explanation of a difficult text of scripture, a short time before his death.

II. My second argument in favor of the use of the Bible in schools, is founded upon an implied command of God, and upon the practice of several of the wisest nations of the world.-In the 6th chapter of Deuteronomy, we find the following words, which are directly to my purpose,

"And thou shalt love the Lord thy God, with thy heart and with all thy soul, and with all thy might. And these words which I command thee this day shall be in thine heart. And thou shalt teach them diligently unto thy children, and shalt talk of them when thou sittest in thine house, and when thou walkest by the way, and when thou liest down, and when thou riseth up."

It appears, moreover, from the history of the Jews, that they flourished as a nation, in proportion as they honored and read the books of Moses, which contained, a written revelation of the will of God, to the children of men. The law was not only neglected, but lost during the general profligacy of manners which accompanied the long and wicked reign of Manasseh. But the discovery of it, in the rubbish of the temple, by Josiah, and its subsequent general use, were followed by a return of national virtue and prosperity. We read further, of the wonderful effects which the reading of the law by Ezra, after his return from his captivity in Babylon, had upon the Jews. They hung upon his lips with tears, and showed the sincerity of their repentance, by their general reformation.

The learning of the Jews, for many years consisted in nothing but a knowledge of the scriptures. These were the text books of all the instruction that was given in the schools of their prophets. It was by means of this general knowledge of their law, that those Jews that wandered from Judea into our countries, carried with them and propagated certain ideas of the true God among all the civilized nations upon the face of the earth. And it was from the attachment they retained to the Old Testament, that they procured a translation of it into the Greek language, after they lost the Hebrew tongue, by their long absence from their native country. The utility of this translation, commonly called the Septuagint, in facilitating the progress of the gospel, is well known to all who are acquainted with the history of the first age of the Christian church.

But the benefits of an early and general acquaintance with the Bible, were not confined only to the Jewish nations. They have appeared in many countries in Europe, since the reformation. The industry, and habits of order, which distinguish many of the German nations, are derived from their early instruction in the principles of Christianity, by means of the Bible. The moral and enlightened character of the inhabitants of Scotland, and of the New England States, appears to be derived from the same cause. If we descend from nations to sects, we shall find them wise and prosperous in proportion as they become early acquainted with the scriptures. The Bible is still used as a schoolbook among the Quakers. The morality of this sect of Christians is universally acknowledged. Nor is this all; their prudence in the management of their private affairs, is as much a mark of their society, as their sober manners.

I wish to be excused for repeating here, that if the Bible did not convey a single direction for the attainment of future happiness, it should be read in our schools in preference to all other books, from its containing the greatest portion of that kind of knowledge which is calculated to produce private and public temporal happiness.

We err not only in human affairs, but in religion likewise, only because "we do not know the scriptures." The opposite systems of the numerous sects of Christians arise chiefly from their being more instructed in catechisms, creeds, and confessions of faith, than in the scriptures. Immense truths, I believe, are concealed in them. The time, I have no doubt, will come, when posterity will view and pity our ignorance of these truths, as much as we do the ignorance of the disciples of our Savior, who knew nothing of the meaning of those plain passages in the Old Testament which were daily fulfilling before their eyes. Whenever that time shall arrive, those truths which have escaped our notice, or if discovered, have been thought to be opposed to each other, or to be inconsistent with themselves, will then like the stones of Solomon's temple, be found so exactly to accord with each other, that they shall be cemented without noise or force, into one simple and sublime system of religion.

But further, we err, not only in religion but in philosophy likewise, because we "do not know or believe "the scriptures." The sciences have been compared to a circle of which religion composes a part. To understand any one of them perfectly it is necessary to have some knowledge of them all. Bacon, Boyle, and Newton included the scriptures in the inquiries to which their universal geniuses disposed them, and their philosophy was aided by their knowledge in them. A striking agreement has been lately discovered between the history of certain events recorded in the Bible and some of the operations and productions of nature, particularly those which are related in Whitehurst's observations on the deluge, in Smith's account of the origin of the variety of color in the human species, and in Bruce's travels. It remains yet to be shown how many other events, related in the Bible, accord with some late important discoveries in the principles of medicine. The events, and the principles alluded to, mutually establish the truth of each other. From the discoveries of the Christian philosophers, whose names have been last mentioned, I have been led to question whether most harm has been done to revelation, by those divines who have unduly multiplied the objects of faith, or by those deists who have unduly multiplied the objects of reason, in explaining the scriptures.

Answering Objections

I shall now proceed to answer some of the objections which have been made to the use of the Bible as a schoolbook.

I. We are told, that the familiar use of the Bible in our schools, has a tendency to lessen a due reverence for it. This objection, by proving too much, proves nothing at all. If familiarity lessens respect for divine things, then all those precepts of our religion, which enjoin the daily or weekly worship of the Deity, are improper. The Bible was not intended to represent a Jewish ark; and it is an anti-Christian idea, to suppose that it can be profaned, by being carried into a schoolhouse, or by being handled by children. But where will the Bible be read by young people with more reverence than in a school? Not in most private families; for I believe there are few parents, who preserve so much order in their houses, as is kept in our common English schools.

II. We are told, that there are many passages in the Old Testament, that are improper to be read by children, and that the greatest part of it is no way interesting to mankind under the present dispensation of the gospel. There are I grant, several chapters, and many verses in the Old Testament, which in their present unfortunate translation, should be passed over by children. But I deny that any of the books of the Old Testament are not interesting to mankind, under the gospel dispensation. Most of the characters, events, and ceremonies, mentioned in them, are personal, providential, or instituted types of the Messiah: All of which have been, or remain yet to be, fulfilled by him. It is from an ignorance or neglect of these types, that we have so many deists in Christendom; for so irrefragably do they prove the truth of Christianity, that I am sure a young man who had been regularly instructed in their meaning, could never doubt afterwards of the truth of any of its principles. If any obscurity appears in these principles, it is only (to use the words of the poet) because they are dark, with excessive bright.

I know there is an objection among many People to teach children doctrines of any kind, because they are liable to be controverted. But where will this objection lead us? The being of a God, and the obligations of morality, have both been controverted; and yet who has objected to our teaching these doctrines to our children?

The curiosity and capacities of young people for the mysteries of religion, awaken much sooner than is generally supposed. Of this we have two remarkable proofs in the Old Testament. The first is mentioned in the twelfth chapter of Exodus:

> And it shall come when your children shall say unto you, "What mean you by this service?" that ye shall say, "It is the sacrifice of the Lord's Passover, who passed over the houses of Israel in Egypt, when he smote the Egyptians, and delivered our houses." And the children of the Israel went away, and did as the Lord had commanded Moses and Aaron.

A second proof of the desire of children to be instructed in the mysteries of religion, is found in the sixth chapter of Deuteronomy.

> And when thy son asketh thee in the time to come saying, "What mean the testimonies and the statutes and the judgements which the Lord our God hath commanded you?" Then thou shalt say unto thy son, "We were Pharaoh's bondmen in Egypt, and the Lord our God brought us out of Egypt with a mighty hand."

These enquiries from the mouths of children are perfectly natural; for where is the parent who has not had similar questions proposed to him by his children upon their being first conducted to a place of worship, and upon their beholding, for the first time, either of the sacraments of our religion?

Let us not be wiser than our Maker. If moral precepts alone could have reformed mankind, the mission of the Son of God into our world, would have been unnecessary. He came to promulgate a system of doctrines, as well as a system of morals. The perfect morality of the gospel rests upon a doctrine, which, though often controverted, has never been refuted, I mean the vicarious life and death of the Son of God. This sublime and ineffable doctrine delivers us from the absurd hypotheses of modern philosophers, concerning the foundation of moral obligation, and fixes it upon the eternal and self-moving principle of LOVE. It concentrates a whole system of ethics in a single text of scripture: "A new commandment I give unto you, that ye love one another, even as I have loved you." By withholding the knowledge of this doctrine from children, we deprive ourselves of the best means of awakening moral sensibility in their minds. We do more, we furnish an argument, for withholding from them a knowledge of the morality of the gospel likewise; for this, in many instances, is as supernatural, and therefore as liable to be controverted, as any of the doctrines or miracles which are mentioned in the New Testament. The miraculous conception of the Savior of the world by a virgin, is not more opposed to the ordinary course of natural events, nor is the doctrine of the atonement more above human reason, than those moral precepts, which command us to love our enemies, or to die for our friends.

III. It has been said, that the division of the Bible into chapters and verses, renders it more difficult to be read, by children than many other books.

By a little care in a master, this difficulty may be obviated, and even an advantage derived from it. It may serve to transfer the attention of the scholar to the sense of a subject; and no person will ever read well, who is guided by anything else, in his stops, emphasis, or accents. The division of the Bible into chapters and verses, is not a greater obstacle to its being read with ease, than the bad punctuation of most other books. I deliver this stricture upon other books, from the authority of Mr. Rice, the celebrated author of the art of speaking, whom I heard declare in a large company in London, that he had never seen a book properly pointed in the English Language. He exemplified, notwithstanding, by reading to the same company a passage from Milton, his perfect knowledge of the art of reading.

Some people, I know, have proposed to introduce extracts from the Bible, into our schools, instead of the Bible itself. Many excellent works of this kind, are in print, but if we admit any one of them, we shall have the same inundation of them that we have had of grammars, spelling books, and lessons for children, many of which are published for the benefit of the authors only, and all of them have tended greatly to increase the expense of education. Besides, these extracts or abridgements of the Bible, often contain the tenets of particular sects or persons, and therefore, may be improper for schools composed of the children of different sects of Christians. The Bible is a cheap book, and is to be had in every bookstore. It is, moreover, esteemed and preferred by all sects; because each finds its peculiar doctrines in it. It should therefore be used in preference to any abridgements of it, or histories extracted from it.

I have heard it proposed that a portion of the Bible should be read every day by the master, as a means of instructing children in it: But this is a poor substitute for obliging children to read it as a schoolbook; for by this means we insensibly engrave, as it were, its contents upon their minds: and it has been remarked that children, instructed in this way in the scriptures, seldom forget any part of them. They have the same advantage over those persons, who have only heard the scriptures read by a master, that a man who has worked with the tools of the mechanical employment for several years, has over the man who has only stood a few hours in a work shop and seen the same business carried on by other people.

In this defense of the use of the Bible as a schoolbook, I beg you would not think that I suppose the Bible to contain the only revelation which God has made to man. I believe in an internal revelation, or a moral principle, which God has implanted in the heart of every man, as the precursor of his final dominion over the whole human race. How much this internal revelation accords with the external, remains yet to be explored by philosophers. I am disposed to believe, that most of the doctrines of Christianity revealed in the Bible might be discovered by a close examination of all the principles of action in man: But who is equal to such an enquiry? It certainly does not suit the natural indolence, or laborious employments of a great majority of mankind. The internal revelation of the gospel may be compared to the straight line which is made through the wilderness by the assistance of a compass, to a distant country, which few are able to discover, while the Bible resembles a public road to the same country, which is wide, plain, and easily found. "And a highway shall be there, and it shall be called the way of holiness. The way faring men, though fools, shall not err therein."

Neither let me in this place exclude the Revelation which God has made of himself to man in the works of creation. I am far from wishing to lessen the influence of this species of Revelation upon mankind. But the knowledge of God obtained from this source, is obscure and feeble in its operation, compared with that which is derived from the Bible. The visible creation speaks of the Deity in hieroglyphics, while the Bible describes all his attributes and perfections in such plain, and familiar language that "he who runs may read."

How kindly has our maker dealt with his creatures, in providing three different cords to draw them to himself! But how weakly do some men act, who suspend their faith, and hopes upon only one of them! By laying hold of them all, they would approach more speedily and certainly to the center of all happiness.

Additional Arguments

To the arguments I have mentioned in favor of the use of the Bible as a schoolbook, I shall add a few reflections.

The present fashionable practice of rejecting the Bible from our schools, I suspect has originated with the deists. They discover great ingenuity in this new mode of attacking Christianity. If they proceed in it, they will do more in half a century, in extirpating our religion, than Bolingbroke or Voltaire could have effected in a thousand years. I am not writing to this class of people. I despair of changing the opinions of any of them. I wish only to alter the opinions and conduct of those lukewarm, or superstitious Christians, who have been misled by the deists upon this subject. On the ground of the good old custom, of using the Bible as a schoolbook, it becomes us to entrench our religion. It is the last bulwark the deists have left it; for they have rendered instruction in the principles of Christianity by the pulpit and the press, so unfashionable, that little good for many years seems to have been done by either of them.

The effects of the disuse of the Bible, as a schoolbook have appeared of late in the neglect and even contempt with which scripture names are treated by many people. It is because parents have not been early taught to know or respect the characters and exploits of the Old and New Testament worthies, that their names are exchanged for those of the modern kings of Europe, or of the principle characters in novels and romances. I conceive there may be some advantage in bearing scripture names. It may lead the persons who bear them, to study that part of the scriptures, in which their names are mentioned, with uncommon attention, and perhaps it may excite a desire in them to possess the talents or virtues of their ancient namesakes. This remark first occurred to me, upon hearing a pious woman whose name was Mary, say, that the first passages of the Bible, which made a serious impression on her mind, were those interesting chapters and verses in which the name of Mary is mentioned in the New Testament.

It is a singular fact, that while the names of the kings and emperors of Rome, are now given chiefly to horses and dogs, scripture names have hitherto been confined only to the human species. Let the enemies and contemners of those names take care, lest the names of more modern kings be given hereafter only to the same animals, and lest the names of the modern heroines of romances be given to animals of an inferior species.

It is with great pleasure, that I have observed the Bible to be the only book read in the Sunday schools in England. We have adopted the same practice in the Sunday schools, lately established in this city. This will give our religion (humanly speaking) the chance of a longer life in our country. We hear much of the persons educated in free schools in England, turning out well in the various walks of life. I have enquired into the cause of it, and have satisfied myself, that it is wholly to be ascribed to the general use of the Bible in those schools, for it seems the children of poor people are of too little consequence to be guarded from the supposed evils of reading the scriptures in early life, or in an unconsecrated school house.

However great the benefits of reading the scriptures in schools have been, I cannot help remarking, that these benefits might be much greater, did schoolmasters take more pains to explain them to their scholars. Did they demonstrate the divine original of the Bible from the purity, consistency, and benevolence of its doctrines and precepts-did they explain the meaning of the Levitical institutions, and show their application to the numerous and successive gospel dispensations-did they inform their pupils that the gross and abominable vices of the Jews were recorded only as proofs of the depravity of human nature, and of the insufficiency of the law, to produce moral virtue and thereby to establish the necessity and perfection of the gospel system-and above all, did they often enforce the discourses of our Savior, as the best rule of life, and the surest guide to happiness, how great would be the influence of our schools upon the order and prosperity of our country! Such a mode of instructing children in the Christian religion, would convey knowledge into their understandings, and would therefore be preferable to teaching them creeds, and catechisms, which too often convey, not knowledge, but words only, into their memories. I think I am not too sanguine in believing, that education, conducted in this manner, would, in the course of two generations, eradicate infidelity from among us, and render civil government scarcely necessary in our country.

In contemplating the political institutions of the United States, I lament, that we waste so much time and money in punishing crimes, and take so little pains to prevent them. We profess to be republicans, and yet we neglect the only means of establishing and perpetuating our republican forms of government, that is the universal education of our youth in the principles of Christianity, by means of the Bible; for this divine book, above all others, favors that equality among mankind, that respect for just laws, and all those sober and frugal virtues, which constitute the soul of republicanism.

I have now only to apologize for having addressed this letter to you, after having been assured by you, that your opinion, respecting the use of the Bible as a schoolbook, coincided with mine. My excuse for what I have done is, that I knew you were qualified by your knowledge, and disposed by your zeal in the cause of truth, to correct all the errors you would discover in my letter. Perhaps a further apology may be necessary for my having presumed to write upon a subject so much above my ordinary studies. My excuse for it is, that I thought a single mite from a member of a profession, which has been frequently charged with skepticism in religion, might attract the notice of persons who had often overlooked the more ample contributions upon this subject, of gentlemen of other professions. With great respect, I am, dear sir, your sincere friend.

BENJAMIN RUSH
Philadelphia, March 10, 1791.

READING 2: PRESIDENT OF CONGRESS STARTS BIBLE SOCIETY

*E*lias Boudinot had been an American patriot, lawyer, and politician who had served as President of the Continental Congress. Though state and local Bible societies had existed as early as 1808, Elias Boudinot possessed a vision for a Bible society that was broader in scope, and in a letter to William Jay, the son of John Jay, America's first Chief Justice of the Supreme Court, Boudinot helped to lay the plans for what

Elias Boudinot

was to become the American Bible Society. More than a month after Boudinot composed his letter to William Jay, a meeting was convened in New York City to organize "a general Bible Society" in America, and on May 11, 1816, the newly formed American Bible Society elected Elias Boudinot as its first president. Boudinot served in this capacity until his death five years later, after which America's first Chief Justice of the United States Supreme Court, John Jay, assumed the presidency.

Prevented by poor health from attending, Elias Boudinot penned a letter to the Board of Managers of the American Bible Society on May 5, 1817. That letter is presented below with the hope that the reader will obtain a deepening appreciation for the Christian spirit of the men and women who birthed America and the character which they hoped to perpetuate within the nation.

Letter from the Honorable Elias Boudinot, President of the American Bible Society

Among the innumerable blessings of this life wherewith it hath pleased a gracious God to favor me, the permitting my union with you in those labors of love, which it is hoped will be made instrumental to the raising a monument to his glory, which may last till the recording angel shall announce to an astonished universe that "it is finished," is one of the most dear to my heart.

The consoling hope was once cherished that the unspeakable pleasure would, in one instance at least, have been afforded me, in the last decline of life, of meeting with you personally, to have testified my approbation of all your exertions in this glorious work. But a kind and merciful God, who knows all my deficiencies, has thought it best, in his infinite wisdom, to refuse this favor, in which dispensation of his all wise Providence I do most sincerely acquiesce, firmly believing it will be most conducive to his own glory and the best interests of the institution committed to our care.

I once thought I had much to communicate to you, but the extreme debility of both mind and body prevents my attempting it. Suffer me, however, as a last effort, however weak and feeble, to say few words before I go hence.

It is not vanity in me to say that I have labored hard and suffered much in this great cause, occasioned is some measure by a very low state of health; yet such has been the apparent interposition of an overruling Providence, that my faith and hope have never failed, even in the darkest days; and although there have been great temptations to despair of final success, yet have I been so strengthened with the assurance that it was a work of God, and that he would show his power and glory in bringing it to maturity in his own time and by his own means, that I had determined, in case of failure in the last attempt, to commence the great business at all events, with the aid of a few laymen who had testified their willingness to go all lengths with me. But no sooner had the work been brought to an issue, than the clouds began to disperse, and every one was obliged to say in his heart, "This is the work of God."

Thus, my beloved friends, hath God in his own condescending grace appointed us to become his humble instruments in opening the eyes of the blind; in cheering the abodes of primeval darkness with the joyful sounds of redeeming love; in fulfilling the encouraging prophecy of the angel flying through the midst of heaven, having the everlasting Gospel in his hands, to preach to all nations, languages, tongues, and people on the earth.

This, indeed, is an event devoutly to be wished, and most gratefully to be acknowledged. That such comparative worms of the dust should become fellow-workers with Christ in making the wilderness to blossom as a rose, and the nations of the earth to become the nations of our Lord and his Christ, is an honor in which the highest angels would rejoice. Is there, then, the least reason for fearing the great result? Shall anyone be discouraged at the arduous prospect before us? By no means. Look at the disciples of our dearest Lord, and compare their relative situation when they beheld their blessed Master given up to the power of his enemies—condemned as a base malefactor—stretched on the cross, breathing out his precious life in a prayer in favor of his unrelenting persecutors—forsaken by all—every one fleeing to his own home, and one even repeatedly denying his Lord and Master, though forewarned of it but a few hours before!

Realize their forlorn state when surrounding the risen Savior, hearkening to his invaluable instructions; he is suddenly parted from them, and carried up into heaven, and vanishes from their sight. It is true, they are commissioned to go forth and preach the Gospel to every creature—a Gospel in all its parts and each essential feature destructive of every religion on the face of the earth. This is to be preached to a world wholly absorbed in the works of the flesh; wholly inimical to the precepts of the meek and holy Jesus—a world in absolute possession of all temporal power and authority. All this is to be done by twelve poor, helpless, indigent, and illiterate fishermen, without power civil or ecclesiastical, friends, influence, riches, or rank to aid them in calling the public attention to their divine Master, who, though declared to be God as well as man, was crucified as a malefactor, condemned by the known judicatories of their country. But will it be said that they had the personal assurance of their Almighty Savior for their encouragement and support against all the powers of earth and hell? Yes, my friends, they had; and a blessed support it was, and under it they withstood and overcame the world. And have you not equal, if not superior cause of trust and hope? Have you not all the promises made to them, with the advantage of their experience and success in the fulfillment of all that he said and did, beyond their most exaggerated expectations? Has your Savior lost his power and authority, or has he not given as much confidence and reliance on his continual presence and almighty arm to you as he ever did to his disciples of old? Is he not the same yesterday, today, and forever?

As for my own part, I have been looking for greater opposition and causes of mortification than any that have yet appeared. I know the seductive power of the evil one, and the artful cunning of his devices. An opposition, indeed, has come from quarters whence we ought not to have expected it; indeed, it has been, as yet, too feeble to excite the fear or cool the zeal of God's people. But, brethren, we are all too well acquainted with the cunning and subtlety of the great enemy of the Gospel to suppose that he will thus early give up his designs. No; but as you have put on the armor of God, you must not put it off till you have obtained a complete, a decided victory. You must be guarded at all points. Woe be to them who shall be the cause of your trouble. Satan's principal endeavors will be to sow divisions among you; he will attack your union, by which you destroy his strong hold, in breaking down the walls of partition that have so long separated and wounded the Church of Christ. He will fear your apparent cordial love and esteem for each other. As long as real brotherly love shall continue and prevail among you, all the arts of the enemy of man's happiness may be defied. Guard well the weakest part of your citadel; forget not the solemn injunction of the captain of your salvation, "By this shall all men know that ye are my disciples, if ye love one another." Stand on your guard; let no argument persuade you; let no vain alarm of danger to your interests intimidate you. Greater is he who is for you than he who is against you. I do know, and have carefully attended to your probable progress. You have an arduous, but a glorious work and labor of love before you; this will necessarily engage all your powers and all your spare time; but look to the great recompense of reward. That you are striving for eternity, not only for yourselves, but for a world lying in sin, who may, at the great day of account, be found surrounding the throne of the Eternal with hallelujahs and thanksgiving, that you were the cause of their coming to the knowledge of the Gospel. Forget not that your Lord and Master has all power given to him, both in heaven and on earth; that under his guardian care—that under the banner of his cross, you are to go forth and complete the triumphs of redeeming love.

Once more suffer me to beseech you to promote love and harmony in your society as your strong bond of union. God is love. Love is the fulfillment of the law. Let it become a common proverb, "See how these members of the American Bible Society love one another, though consisting of every denomination of Christians among us." Let a motto be written in letters of gold on the most prominent part of your hall of deliberation, "By this shall all men know ye are my disciples, if ye love one another." If this, then, is the great characteristic mark of discipleship with Christ, who will refuse to wear the badge as the most desirable trait in his character? The second advent of the Savior is comparatively near—the harbingers of his approach begin to appear. Hear the language of Jesus himself: "For the Son of Man shall come in the glory of his Father, with his angels; and then shall he reward every man according to his works. Hereafter ye shall see the Son of Man sitting on the right hand of power, and coming in the clouds of heaven with power and great glory." St. Paul commendeth the Thessalonians for their faith Godward, and waiting for his Son from heaven. "For this we say unto you, by the words of the Lord, If we believe that Jesus died and rose again, even so (as certainly) they also who sleep in Jesus will God bring with him, for this we say unto you, by the word of the Lord, that the Lord himself shall descend from heaven with a shout, with the voice of the Archangel, and the dead in Christ shall rise first." I rejoice with you, that to accomplish this glorious end, to hasten this blessed event, and to become fellow workers with God, we are assisting in laying the foundation for spreading the Gospel throughout the habitable globe, that the earth may be covered with the knowledge of God as the waters cover the seas, when we may all sit down with Abraham, Isaac, and Jacob in the kingdom of our Lord.

And now, brethren, beloved in the Lord, I commit you to the grace of that God who hath preserved my life to my seventy eighth year as a living monument of his sparing mercy and goodness, to witness your zeal, activity, and perseverance in his service. May the broad hand of the Almighty cover you; may his Holy Spirit guide, direct, and influence you in all your deliberations and undertakings, and make you burning and shining lights in his Israel. And when the great Shepherd of the sheepfold shall call in his ancient people, the Jews, from the four quarters of the world, may you be found among the number of those who shall he made kings and priests to God.

And now, my beloved friends and brethren, suffer me to leave you, under the pleasing expectation that we shall meet again, to unite in that song of everlasting praise that shall proceed from the trump of the archangel, when he shall sound the glorious anthem of hallelujah! hallelujah! hallelujah! for the Lord God Omnipotent reigneth.

Soli Dei Gloria et Honor.

Elias Boudinot, President
To the Board of Managers of the American Bible Society
Burlington, 5th May, 1817[135]

---

[135] W Strickland, *History of the American Bible Society From Its Organization to the Present Time* (New York: Harper & Bros., 1849), 349-352.

READING 3: BY THE BIBLE OR BY THE BAYONET

*R*obert Winthrop rose to the position of Speaker of the United States House of Representatives and was an advocate of Bible societies and their ministry to America. As was characteristic of many Founding Fathers, Winthrop involved himself in the advancement of Christianity in America—particularly through his political influence, oratory, literary endeavors, and the distribution of the Bible. He is widely

Robert Winthrop

remembered for an address he delivered at the Annual Meeting of the Massachusetts Bible Society in Boston on May 28, 1849. In his address, Winthrop noted a common theme among America's Founding Fathers concerning the importance of self-government, the principles for which— they believed—were best found in the Bible. He argued, we must be governed by "the Bible or by the bayonet." Speaker Winthrop's address is presented below in its entirety.

The Bible
An Address Delivered at the Annual Meeting of
The Massachusetts Bible Society
In Boston, MAY 28, 1849.

In rising to move the adoption of the report which has just been read, I feel deeply, Mr. President, how apt I shall be to disappoint any part of the expectations of this meeting, which may, by any chance, have been directed towards myself. I have not come here this afternoon in the hope of saying anything which might not be better said by others more accustomed to deal with occasions of this sort; or anything, indeed, which has not been, a hundred times already, better said by those who have heretofore taken part in these Anniversary celebrations.

But I was unwilling to refuse any service which your committee of arrangements might even imagine me capable of rendering to the cause in which you are assembled. I could not find it in my conscience, or in my heart, to decline bearing my humble testimony, whenever and wherever it might be called for, to the transcendent interest and importance of the object for which this Association has now lived and labored for the considerable period of forty years.

That object is the publication and general distribution of the Holy Scriptures; and no man, I am sure, who has had the privilege of listening to the report of my Reverend friend, (Dr. Parkman,) and who has a soul capable of appreciating the grandeur of those aggregate results which he has so well set forth, can fail to pronounce it one of the greatest, most important, most comprehensive and catholic objects, to which human means and human efforts have ever been devoted.

The week on which we have just entered, has been signalized, I had almost said hallowed, among us, for many years past, by the meetings of many noble associations; and a record of philanthropy and charity has been annually presented to us in their reports and addresses, which must have filled every benevolent bosom with joy. But it has been a most appropriate and significant arrangement, that this Society should take the lead in these Anniversary festivals. Undoubtedly, Sir, the first of all charities, the noblest of all philanthropies, is that which brings the Bible home to every fireside, which places its Divine truths within the range of every eye, and its blessed promises and consolations within the reach of every heart.

All other charities should follow, and, indeed, they naturally do follow, in the train of this. Let the great work of this Association be thoroughly prosecuted and successfully accomplished, and the soil will be prepared, and the seed sown, for a golden and glorious harvest.

Diffuse the knowledge of the Bible, and the hungry will be fed, and the naked clothed. Diffuse the knowledge of the Bible, and the stranger will be sheltered, the prisoner visited, and the sick ministered unto. Diffuse the knowledge of the Bible, and Temperance will rest upon a surer basis than any mere private pledge or public statute. Diffuse the knowledge of the Bible, and the peace of the world will be secured by more substantial safeguards than either the mutual fear, or the reciprocal interests, of princes or of people. Diffuse the knowledge of the Bible, and the day will be hastened, as it can be hastened in no other way, when every yoke shall be loosened, and every bond broken, and when there shall be no more leading into captivity.

It is the influence of the Bible, in a word, by which the very fountains of philanthropy must be unsealed, and all the great currents of human charity set in motion. It is here alone that we can find the principles, the precepts, the examples, the motives, the rewards, by which men can be effectually moved to supply the wants and relieve the sufferings of their fellow-men, and to recognize the whole human race as members of a common family, and children of a common Parent.

Is it not the Bible, Sir, which teaches us that "to visit the fatherless and widows in their affliction," is as vital a part of pure and undefiled religion, as "to keep ourselves unspotted from the world?" Is it not the Bible which instructs us, that while" to love God with all our heart is the first and great commandment," "to love our neighbor as our self is the second and like unto it?" Is it not the Bible which charges "those who are rich in this world, that they be ready to give and glad to distribute, laying up for themselves a good foundation against the time to come, that they may attain eternal life?"

Is it not plain, then, Mr. President, that the original moving spring, and the still sustaining power, of that whole system of moral and religious machinery, whose grand results are so proudly exhibited to us during this anniversary week, must be found in the promulgation and diffusion of the Holy Scriptures? May we not fairly say, without arrogance on our own part or disparagement towards others, that all other benevolent associations are but distributors and service-pipes (if I may so speak) to that great Reservoir of living waters, over which this Association has assumed the special guardianship, and which it is its chosen and precious province to keep fresh, and full, and free to all the world?

Even this, however, I am aware, Sir, is but a single and a somewhat subordinate aspect of the great work in which you are engaged. Indeed, as we hold up this subject in the sunlight before our eyes, we find a thousand other views of its interest and importance multiplying and brightening around us, as in a prism.

Regarded only as a mere human and utterly uninspired composition, (if, indeed, it be possible for any one so to regard it,) who can over-estimate, who can adequately appreciate, the value of the Bible as a book for general circulation, reading, and study? I remember to have seen it somewhere mentioned, that in an old English Statute of about the year 1516, — I doubt not that you, Mr. President,[136] could tell us the precise date of its passage,— the sacred volume, instead of being denominated *Biblion* the book, was called *Bibliotheca*, — the library. And what a library it must have been in that early day of English literature! Nay, what a library it still is to us all now! Within what other covers have ever been comprised such diversified stores of entertainment and instruction, such inexhaustible mines of knowledge and wisdom!

---

[136] Hon. Simon Greenleaf occupied the Chair.

The oldest of all books, as in part it certainly is; the most common of all books, as the efforts of these associations have now undoubtedly made it; how truly may we say of it, that "age cannot wither, nor custom stale its infinite variety!" The world, which seems to outgrow successively all other books, finds still in this an ever fresh adaptation to every change in its condition and every period in its history. Now, as a thousand years ago, it has lessons alike for individuals and for nations; for rulers and for people; for monarchies and for republics; for times of stability and for times of overthrow; for the rich and the poor; for the simplest and the wisest.

Whatever is most exquisite in style, whatever is most charming in narrative, whatever is most faithful in description, whatever is most touching in pathos, whatever is most sublime in imagery, whatever is most marvelous in incident, whatever is most momentous in import, find here alike and always their unapproached and unapproachable original.

It was but a day or two since that I was reading that the great German poet, Goethe, had said of the little book of Ruth, that there was nothing so lovely in the whole range of epic or idyllic poetry. It was but yesterday that I was reading the tribute of the no less distinguished Humboldt to the matchless fidelity and grandeur of the Hebrew lyrics, in the course of which he speaks of a single Psalm (the 104th) as presenting a picture of the entire Cosmos. I have heard that our own Fisher Ames, who has left behind him a reputation for eloquence hardly inferior to that of any American orator either of his own day or of ours, was accustomed to say that he owed more of the facility and felicity of his diction to the Bible, and particularly to the book of Deuteronomy, than to any other source, ancient or modern.

Indeed, Sir, the art, the literature, and the eloquence of all countries and of all times, have united in paying a common homage to the Bible. It has inspired the noblest strains of music and the loftiest triumphs of the painter. Where would be the harmonies of the great composers, where would be the galleries of the old masters, without the subjects with which the Bible has supplied them?

Other books, I know, both in ancient and modern times, have received striking tributes to their genius, their ability, their novelty, their fascination. It will never be forgotten by the admirers of Homer, that Alexander the Great carried the Iliad always about with him in a golden casket. It will never be forgotten by the eulogists of Grotius, that Gustavus Adolphus, in the war which he waged in Germany for the liberty of Protestant Europe, slept always with the treatise *De Jure Belli ac Pacis* on his pillow. But how many caskets and how many pillows have borne testimony to the Bible! Yes, Sir, of heroes and conquerors, not less mighty than the Macedonian or the Swede; and not of those only who have been called to wrestle against flesh and blood, but of those who have contended "against principalities and powers, against the rulers of the darkness of this world, against spiritual wickedness in high places," and who have found in this holy volume, as in the very armory of Heaven, "the sword of the Spirit, the breastplate of righteousness, the helmet of salvation, and the shield of faith, by which they have been able to quench all the fiery darts of the wicked."

I perceive, Mr. President, how impossible it is to separate the influence of the Bible as a mere book, from that which it owes to its divine character and origin. And they ought not to be separated. Unquestionably, it is as containing the word of God, the revelation of immortality, the gospel of salvation, that the Bible presents its preeminent title to the affection and reverence of the world. And it is in this view above all others, that its universal distribution becomes identified with the highest temporal and eternal interests of the human race.

I say, with the highest temporal, as well as eternal interests of the human race; and I desire to dwell for a single moment longer, on the inseparable connection of the work in which this and other kindred associations are engaged, with the advancement of civilization, with the elevation of mankind, and with the establishment and maintenance of free institutions. I desire, especially, to express the opinion, which I have been led of late to cherish daily and deeply, that everything in the character of our own institutions, and everything in the immediate condition of our own country, calls for the most diligent employment of all the moral and religious agencies within our reach, and particularly for increased activity in the distribution of the Bible.

Mr. President, there is a striking coincidence of dates in the history of our country, and in the history of the Bible. You remember that it was about the year 1607, that King James the First, of blessed memory for this if for nothing else, gave it in charge to fifty or sixty of the most learned ministers of his realm, to prepare that version of the Holy Scriptures, which is now everywhere received and recognized among Protestant Christians as the Bible. This version was finally published in 1611, and it is from this event that the general diffusion of the Bible may fairly be said to date.

The Bible had, indeed, been more than once previously translated and previously printed. During the two preceding centuries, there had been Wickliff's version, and Tyndale's version, and Coverdale's version, and Cranmer's version, and the Geneva Bible, and the Douay Bible, and I know not what others; and they had all been more or less extensively circulated and read, in manuscript or in print, in churches and in families, sometimes under the sanction, and sometimes in defiance of the civil and spiritual authorities.

I doubt not that many of my hearers will remember the vivid picture which Dr. Franklin has given us, in his autobiography, of the manner in which the Bible was read during a portion of this period. Some of his progenitors, it seems, in the days of bloody Mary, were the fortunate possessors of an English Bible, and to conceal it the more securely, they were driven, he tells us "to the project of fastening it open with pack threads across the leaves, on the inside of the lid of the close-stool."

"When my great-grandfather (he proceeds) wished to read the Bible to his family, he reversed the lid of the stool upon his knees, and passed the leaves from one side to the other, which were held down on each by the pack thread. One of the children was stationed at the door to give notice if he saw the proctor (an officer of the spiritual court) make his appearance; in that case, the lid was restored to its place, with the Bible concealed under it as before."

It is plain, that however precious the Bible must have been to those who possessed it in those days, and however strong the influence which it may have exerted over individual minds, it had little chance to manifest its power over the masses, under circumstances like these. Indeed, the whole number of printed Bibles in existence in Great Britain, up to the commencement of the seventeenth century, is estimated at only about one hundred and seventeen thousand; a little more than one fifth the number distributed by the American Bible Society, and only a little more than one tenth the number distributed by the British and Foreign Bible Society, during the single year last past.

It is, thus, only from the publication of the authorized and standard version of King James, that the general diffusion of the Holy Scriptures can be said to have commenced. It was then that the printed word of God " first began to have free course and to be glorified." And that, you remember, Mr. President, was the very date of the earliest settlement of these North American Colonies. It was just then, that the Cavaliers were found planting themselves at Jamestown in Virginia; and it was just then, that the Pilgrims, with the Bible in their hands, were seen flying over to Leyden, on their way to our own Plymouth Rock.

And now, Sir, it is not more true, in my judgment, that the first settlement of our country was precisely coincident in point of time, with the preparation and publication of this standard version of the Bible, than it is that our free institutions have owed their successful rise and progress thus far, and are destined to owe their continued security and improvement in time to come, to the influences which that preparation and publication could alone have produced.

The voice of experience and the voice of our own reason speak but one language on this point. Both unite in teaching us, that men may as well build their houses upon the sand and expect to see them stand, when the rains fall, and the winds blow, and the floods come, as to found free institutions upon any other basis than that morality and virtue, of which the Word of God is the only authoritative rule, and the only adequate sanction.

All societies of men must be governed in some way or other. The less they may have of stringent state government the more they must have of individual self-government. The less they rely on public law or physical force, the more they must rely on private moral restraint. Men, in a word, must necessarily be controlled, either by a power within them, or by a power without them; either by the word of God, or by the strong arm of man; either by the Bible, or by the bayonet. It may do for other countries and other governments to talk about the state supporting religion. Here, under our own free institutions, it is religion which must support the state.

And never more loudly than at this moment have these institutions of ours called for such support. The immense increase of our territorial possessions, with the wild and reckless spirit of adventure which they have brought with them; the recent discovery of the gold mines of California, with the mania for sudden acquisition, for "making haste to be rich," which it has everywhere excited; the vast annual accession to our shores of nearly half a million of foreigners, so many of whom are without any other notion of liberty, at the outset than as the absence of all restraint upon their appetites and passions; who does not perceive in all these circumstances that our country is threatened, more seriously than it ever has been before, with that moral deterioration, which has been the unfailing precursor of political downfall? And who is so bold a believer in any system of human checks and balances as to imagine, that dangers like these can be effectively counteracted or averted in any other way, than by bringing the mighty moral and religious influences of the Bible to bear in our defense.

As patriots, then, no less than as Christians, Mr. President, I feel that we are called upon to unite in the good work of this Association. And let us rejoice that it is a work in which we can all join hands without hesitation or misgiving. There is no room here, I thank heaven, for differences of parties or of sects. There is no room here for controversies about systems or details. Your machinery is of all others the most simple. Your results are of all others the most certain. In a period of little more than forty years, by the agency of associations like this, more than thirty-five millions of Bibles and Testaments have been distributed throughout the world, and more than six millions of them within the limits of our own land. Let us persevere in this noble enterprise. And let each one of us resolve to secure for himself, against the hour which sooner or later must come to us all, that consolation which I doubt not is at this moment cheering the decline of your late venerable President (Dr. Pierce,) — the consolation of reflecting, that it has not been for the want of any proportionate contributions or proportionate efforts on our part, if every human being has not had a Bible to live by, and a Bible to die by.

Selected Works

The First Report of the Bible Society, Established in Philadelphia Read before the Society at Their Annual Meeting, May 1, 1809: With an Appendix and a List of Subscribers and Benefactors. Philadelphia: Printed by order of the Society; Fry and Kammerer printers, 1809.

Journals of the Continental Congress, 1774-1789. 34 vols., edited by Worthington C. Ford and et al. Washington, D.C.: Government Printing Office, 1904.

"The First Charter of Virginia; April 10, 1606." Yale Law School, Lillian Goldman Law Library. Last modified Accessed July 6, 2015. http://avalon.law.yale.edu/17th_century/va01.asp.

Asbury, Francis. *The Journal and Letters of Francis Asbury.* edited by Elmer T. Clark. Nashville: Abingdon Press, 1958.

Beecher, Lyman and Charles Beecher. *Autobiography, Correspondence, Etc., of Lyman Beecher, D.D.* New York: Harper, 1864.

Boehm, Henry. *The Patriarch of One Hundred Years Being Reminiscences, Historical and Biographical, of Rev. Henry Boehm.* 1982 reprint ed. New York: Nelson & Phillips, 1875.

Bradford, William. *Of Plymouth Plantation: Bradford's History of the Plymouth Settlement, 1608-1650.* Bulverde TX: Mantle Ministries, 1998.

Cousins, Norman. *"In God We Trust"; the Religious Beliefs and Ideas of the American Founding Fathers.* 1ˢᵗ ed. New York: Harper, 1958.

Federer, William J. . *The Original 13: A Documentary History of Religion in America's First Thirteen States.* St. Louis, MO: Amerisearch, Inc., 2007.

Franklin, Benjamin. *The Autobiography of Benjamin Franklin with Notes and a Sketch of Franklin's Life from the Point Where the Autobiography Ends, Drawn Chiefly from His Letters.* Boston: Houghton, Mifflin and Company, 1888.

Galloway, Charles B. *Christianity and the American Commonwealth: The Influence of Christianity in Making This Nation.* Reprint ed. Powder Springs, Georgia: American Vision, 2005.

Hyneman, Charles S. and Donald S. Lutz. *American Political Writing During the Founding Era, 1760-1805.* 2 vols. Indianapolis: Liberty Press, 1983.

Jefferson, Thomas. *Notes on the State of Virginia.* A New Edition ed. Richmond, VA: J. W. Randolph, 1853.

Kramnick, Isaac and R. Laurence Moore. *The Godless Constitution: The Case against Religious Correctness.* 1ˢᵗ ed. New York: Norton, 1996.

Lossing, B. J. *Signers of the Declaration of Independence.* New York: Geo. F. Cooledge, 1848.

Lutz, Donald S. *The Origin of American Constitutionalism.* Baton Rouge: Louisiana State University Press, 1988.

Millard, Catherine. *The Rewriting of America's History.* Camp Hill, PA: Horizon House Publishers, 1991.

Mitchell, Thomas. *The Character of Rush: An Introductory to the Course on the Theory and Practice of Medicine, in the Philadelphia College of Medicine.* Philadelphia [Pa.]: John H. Gihon Printer, 1848.

Orr, J. Edwin. *The Eager Feet: Evangelical Awakenings, 1790-1830.* Chicago: Moody Press, 1975.

Pennsylvania Society for Promoting the Abolition of Slavery. *Centennial Anniversary of the Pennsylvania Society, for Promoting the Abolition of Slavery, the Relief of Free Negroes Unlawfully Held in Bondage: And for Improving the Condition of the African Race.* Philadelphia: Grant, Faires & Rodgers, printers, 1875.

Ramsay, David. *An Eulogium Upon Benjamin Rush, M.D., Professor of the Institutes and Practice of Medicine and of Clinical Practice in the University of Pennsylvania. Who Departed This Life April 19, 1813, in the Sixty-Ninth Year of His Age. Written at the Request of the Medical Society of South Carolina, and Delivered before Them and Others, in the Circular Church of Charleston, on the 10th of June, 1813, and Pub. At Their Request.* Phildelphia: Bradford and Inskeep, 1813.

Sanderson, John. *Biography of the Signers to the Declaration of Independence.* 4 vols. Philadelphia: R. W. Pomeroy, 1823.

Sparks, Jared. *The Writings of George Washington; Being His Correspondence, Addresses, Messages, and Other Papers, Official and Private, Selected and Published from the Original Manuscripts; with a Life of the Author, Notes, and Illustrations.* 12 vols. Boston: Little, Brown, 1858.

Washington, George. "George Washington to Meshech Weare, Et Al, June 8, 1783, Circular Letter of Farewell to Army." Library of Congress. Last modified Accessed January 2, 2016. http://memory. loc.gov/cgi-bin/query/r?ammem/mgw:@field%28DOCID+@ lit%28gw260534%29%29.

CPSIA information can be obtained
at www.ICGtesting.com
Printed in the USA
LVOW10s0428020217

522933LV00011B/33/P